BLACK AMERICA SERIES

POLITICS, CIVIL RIGHTS, AND LAW IN BLACK ATLANTA 1870–1970

Herman "Skip" Mason, Jr.

ARCADIA

Copyright © 2000 by Herman "Skip" Mason, Jr.
ISBN 0-7524-0985-9

Published by Arcadia Publishing,
an imprint of Tempus Publishing, Inc.
2 Cumberland Street
Charleston, SC 29401

Printed in Great Britain.

Library of Congress Catalog Card Number: 00-102961

For all general information contact Arcadia Publishing at:
Telephone 843-853-2070
Fax 843-853-0044
E-Mail sales@arcadiapublishing.com

For customer service and orders:
Toll-Free 1-888-313-2665

Visit us on the internet at http://www.arcadiaimages.com

Rev. Martin Luther King, Jr. (seated) confers with Rev. William Holmes Borders at a mass rally at the Wheat Street Baptist Church, c. 1961.

CONTENTS

Acknowledgments

This publication is dedicated to all of the known and unknown persons who sacrificed their lives to obtain our inalienable rights of life, liberty, and the pursuit of happiness. I am especially grateful to Dr. Albert Davis (who brought me into this world), an advocate for the injustices of the medical community in Atlanta, and "Mama" Jondelle Johnson (former executive director of the NAACP) who blazed a fiery path in her pursuit of justice for all people. A very special thanks to Dr. Herman Reese, for his years of support, mentoring, and an occasional tongue-lashing, and to Mrs. Mary Elizabeth Hawk, who taught me that "Culture is the continuous changing patterns of learned behavior. The products of learned behavior included knowledge, attitude and material gains which are shared and transmitted among the makers of society." Thanks also go to Casper Leroy Jordan, another mentor; my uncle Henry Harris Jr.; and cousins Drs. Lorene and Paul Brown and Pat Perry, for their continued support. As always, I am grateful to my close and extended families, especially the loving support and encouragement of my wife, Harmel, my mother, Deloris Hughes, my late father, Herman "Pop" Mason, Arthur Conley, and sisters Dionne and Minyon Conley. As always, this and other publications are done for the nieces, Kenyondra, Shakari, and JoLaun, and my unborn child, who should arrive at about the time this book is published.

I am very grateful to my former students at Morehouse College, fall 1997, for their assistance with this project, namely Jibril Akbar, Mutaquee Akbar, De'Shawn Branch, William H. Cade II, Dash Cooper, Derek Cooper, Omoruyi Evbuoma, Glenn E. Fleming, Scotti Gladney, Franklin Goldwire, Rory "Dee" Griffin, Chadwick Johnson, DeAngelo Little, Shamal Mason, Aaron Merriweather, Eulus Moore, Carlton Owens, Joseph Parker, Efrain Reyes, Derrick Robicheaux, Eric Saxon, Kelly M. Smith III., Ozzie Smith, Rahmin Smith, Mark Stevens, Willie Vasher, and Scott A. Wicker.

Finally, to my Morris Brown College, Greater Hopewell CME Church, Alpha Phi Alpha, and Therrell High School families, I thank you for your continued prayers and support.

INTRODUCTION

Atlanta, my hometown, may not be the cradle of the Civil Rights Movement according to most major historians, but it is clear that we cradled, from infancy, the most recognized icon of the movement, Dr. Martin Luther King, Jr. However, this publication is not solely about Dr. King, for preceding Dr. King and following his death, major strides and gains were made in the civil rights of black Atlanta. There is a virtually untold story of the quest of African Americans in Atlanta to undo the evil injustices of a segregated society through community activism, legal gains, and political accomplishments.

Politics, Civil Rights, and Law in Black Atlanta examines the events, movements, and individuals who worked toward creating that "beloved community" where men and women were not judged by the color of the skin but the content of their character.

As with most of my books, photographic images are used to help illustrate the story and capture, in some instances, persons who probably would not be included in any book and events where the images speak for themselves. Much research has been done to ensure historical and factual details regarding African Americans' quest to break the political barriers. It is hoped that this book will help to rekindle memories for some and to acquaint others with some rich historic moments such as the 1920 NAACP Convention and the 1944 Massive Voter Registration drive. Can you imagine the pride in black Atlantans' hearts when they stood outside of the Butler Street YMCA in April of 1948 to witness the first eight African-American policemen or, in 1962, the first 16 African-American firemen. How some of the oldtimers must have felt when Leroy Johnson raised his hand to take the oath as the first African-American state senator since Reconstruction.

Over the last decade, numerous books have been published on the Civil Rights Movement of the South. From Birmingham to Montgomery, the movement has been chronicled in pictures, text, historical documentaries, and major motion picture films. This publication seeks to document African Americans in a quest for political gains and the often fiery movement behind it. For many people, Atlanta's movement is often linked solely to activities and actions of its native son, Rev. Dr. Martin Luther King, Jr. But as NAACP president and former SNCC president Julian Bond said, "He was not alone." This publication, in a very small way, attempts to remember those persons and events whose work and labor have not gone unnoticed.

The Civil Rights Movement in the United States was a legal, political, and social struggle by blacks to get their full rights as citizens and, also, to achieve racial equality. Segregation, the laws and customs separating blacks and whites that were used by whites to control blacks, was a major problem during the early to mid-1900s and was the main focus of the Civil Rights Movement. Individuals and civil rights organizations challenged discrimination and segregation with protest marches, a refusal to abide by segregation laws, and boycotts. The Montgomery bus boycott in 1955 is believed to be the beginning of the movement, with the ending being the Voting Rights Act of 1965.

With segregation came an attempt to achieve complete dominance and supremacy over blacks. Segregation was the norm in most places in the United States, and after the Reconstruction, the Democratic Party gained control of Southern states' governments. The

Democratic Party reversed many of the advances made by blacks during Reconstruction. Segregation laws were passed that put blacks in separate schools, transportation, parks, and restaurants. The black facilities were very inferior to those of whites, and "Jim Crow" laws separated the races in every possible way.

The Civil Rights Movement was fundamental in many cities, including Atlanta. Atlanta was a blooming city that was home to many blacks during the time frame of the Civil Rights Movement. It was growing in its importance, and its population has been steadily increasing. Because of the fact that Atlanta contained the Atlanta University Center, which was over 95 percent black, Atlanta had more black professionals than any other Southern city. Atlanta was, because of its extremely large black population, the perfect spot for the Civil Rights Movement.

The college students in the South, including Atlanta, held sit-ins to express their dislike of the Jim Crow laws. Black students used these sit-ins to express their yearning for equality. The sit-in movement began on February 1, 1960, in Greensboro, NC, when a small group of students refused to leave a store that did not cater to blacks. A few days later, students from black schools throughout the South were talking of hosting demonstrations of their own. The students sent out proposals to different important figures in Atlanta, asking for their support. The appeal the students wrote was very eloquent, and it surprised many whites. It stated the following:

> The time has come for the people of Atlanta and Georgia to take a good look at what is really happening in this country, and to stop believing those who tell us that everything is fine and equal, and that the Negro is happy and satisfied . . . We must say in all candor that we plan to use every legal and nonviolent means at our disposal to secure full citizenship rights as members of this great democracy of ours.

The proposal invoked mixed reactions; the mayor of Atlanta at the time of the proposal, William Hartsfield, gave his support to the protests, stating that it was "a message of great importance to Atlanta" and expressed "the legitimate aspirations of young people throughout the nation and the entire world." The governor of Atlanta at the time, Ernest Vandiver, however, had a totally different view. He thought that the statement was too skillful to be made by blacks, especially students, and that it had overtones suggesting it was anti-American propaganda. The governor said that it was a left-wing statement made to breed "dissatisfaction, discontent and evil." The sit-ins began March 15 so that the seriousness and momentum of previous sit-ins in other states would not be forgotten. They helped to intensify the Civil Rights Movement and to convey its importance.

The sit-ins were just one of many methods used by blacks during their struggle for equality. Lester Maddox, who would become governor of Georgia two years later, kicked a black man out of his establishment after the Civil Rights Act of 1964 was passed. Maddox received plenty of flak for this and finally was forced to serve blacks. Many whites held the same view as Maddox, and there was plenty of racial tension in the air. After King won the Nobel Peace Prize in the fall of 1964, a bi-racial dinner was held in his honor. This was another event that helped with racial equality. It came on the heels of the Civil Rights Act of 1964 and was key to the desegregation of many Atlanta businesses.

The Civil Rights Movement thrived in Atlanta, as it did it many of the cities where blacks held power. With the help of the sit-ins, Martin Luther King, Jr., and others, Atlanta's movement was a success and important to the overall movement of the country. The blacks in Atlanta helped to show that they had a voice and would not go away easily. They expected—no, deserved—the same rights and freedom as whites and would peacefully demand that their needs be met fully on the matter. There was no middle ground—they wanted equality, which would not occur without desegregation and enforcement of the new Civil Rights laws.

One

SEPARATE AND UNEQUAL: 1865–1920

"I shall neither fawn nor cringe before any party, nor stoop to beg for my rights.
I am here to demand my rights, and hurl thunderbolts at the men
who dare cross the threshold of my manhood.

—Henry McNeal Turner

One of the first vocal social activists in Atlanta was the fiery Henry McNeal Turner. Turner was born free on February 1, 1834, in Newberry, SC. His teenage mother, Sarah Turner, and maternal grandmother, Hannah Greer, raised him. His father, Hardy Turner, was not around because he died while Henry was a child. Henry's maternal grandmother had considerable pride in the African race, which she conveyed to her grandson at an early age. She once told him a story that indicated that people of color must use the power of the written word when fighting the oppression inflicted by whites. She said, "when God first made the different races he concluded to try three kinds first as an experiment, the white man, Indian, and Negro. God informed these men that they must work for a living and gave them a choice between three kinds of tools: plow and hoe, bow and arrow, and pen and ink. The black man quickly selected the agriculture implements, while the Indian grabbed the bow and arrow, leaving the pen and ink to the slow-moving white man, who misused them in an attempt to prove that the Negro is his by an unalterable law. When the black man challenged this conclusion; but ere he winds up two or more whites come in and swear by their Alpha and Omega that every word is true. Mr. Negro goes under, as a natural consequence, and rises no more. Thus you see the pen is mightier than the sword." This story is actually saying that if blacks ever hoped to outthink whites, they needed to learn to read and

write in order to defend themselves against such devilish schemes. This was essential to Turner's thinking throughout his life.

At the early age of 12, Turner had a dream that millions of people would come to him for instruction and that he would teach them while standing on a mountain. He knew then that it was his mission in life to be a leader. He understood that literacy would be very important for his future vocation. During this time, many laws were enforced that prohibited the teaching of reading or writing to blacks. The gift of learning was given to him when he was hired as a room sweeper by a law firm in Abbeville, SC. The lawyers educated him in arithmetic, astronomy, geography, history, law, and theology. His knowledge, acquired from educating himself and from others, such as the lawyers, educating him, was instrumental in his preparation for his chosen career as a minister and educator.

Turner had a rapid advancement in the African Methodist Episcopal (AME) denomination from 1858 to 1865. He was the pastor of two small churches in Baltimore (1858–60); Union Bethel Church in Baltimore (1860–62); and Israel Church in Washington, D.C. (1862–63). He was ordained a deacon in April 1860, and two years later, the higher status of elder was granted to him. He left the regular pastorate of the AME Church in June 1863 in order to become a chaplain in the Union army.

During the Civil War, President Abraham Lincoln appointed him as chaplain of the 54th Massachusetts Regiment. In 1868, he was elected to the state legislature and opposed the successful attempt of white lawmakers to expel and remove the legislators of African-American descent. A staunch Republican, he and other African-American Republicans were driven from the Georgia House of Representatives and were reseated by order of Congress. Turner was reelected twice after the United States Supreme Court dissolved the Civil Rights Act of 1875. Turner raged that the Constitution was "a dirty rag, a cheat, a libel, and ought to be spit upon by every Negro in the land." He became one of the first Pan Africanists and colonizationists and protested the violent actions of the Klu Klux Klan. From 1880 to 1915 he was a bishop in the AME Church. "He was a forerunner of the modern civil rights and black power movements," according to Stephen Ward Angell. Turner was one of the most skillful denominational builders in United States history, and was one of the people responsible for the growth of the AME Church in the South.

Bishop Henry McNeal Turner died at the age of 81 in Windsor, Canada. Several churches in Atlanta and a former high school, now a middle school, are named in his honor.

William Finch, born near Athens, GA, was a former slave who was trained as a tailor and operated a successful business on Peachtree Street. A member of the Republican party, Finch was elected as the first African American to serve on the Atlanta City Council in 1871 as a representative of the Fourth Ward (a predominately black area of Atlanta), along with George Graham. They were elected December 7, 1870, took the oath of office on January 7, 1871, and served one year. Finch proposed a city law concerning public school education that greatly influenced the public educational system.

Abraham Lincoln's success in the Civil War and the end of slavery sparked a new era for the black race in the United States. Although the "Black Codes" passed following the Civil War guaranteed blacks their freedom from slavery, the law segregated them from whites. Segregation sparked questions about the rights guaranteed in the 14th amendment, questions that would become a significant factor in a lawsuit 28 years after the amendment was adopted.

In 1890, Louisiana passed a statute providing "that all railway companies carrying passengers in their coaches in this state shall provide equal but separate accommodation for the White and Colored races, by providing two or more passengers coaches for each passenger train, or by dividing the passenger coaches by a partition so as to secure separate accommodations." The penalty for sitting in the wrong compartment was either a fine of $25 or 20 days in jail. On June 7, 1892, Homer Plessy, a 30-year-old shoemaker, was jailed for sitting in the "white's" car of the East Louisiana Railroad between New Orleans and Covington. The irony of the whole case was that Plessy was a mix of seven-eighths white and one-eighth black, but Louisiana law still considered him black and therefore required him to sit in the "colored" car.

Plessy went to court and argued that the separate car act violated the 13th and 14th Amendments. The judge, John Howard Ferguson, had previously declared the Separate Car Act "unconstitutional on trains that traveled through several states." However, in regard to the Plessy trial, he stated that Louisiana could regulate railroad companies that only operated within its state. Ferguson found Plessy guilty. Plessy decided to appeal the decision to the Louisiana State Supreme Court, and it upheld Ferguson's decision. Plessy then took his case to the United States Supreme Court. In 1896, the Supreme Court of the United States found Homer Plessy guilty. Justice Henry Brown, the speaker for the eight-person majority, wrote the following:

> That [the Separate Car Act] does not conflict with the Thirteenth Amendment, which abolished slavery.is too clear for argument. A stature which implies merely a legal distinction between the white and the colored races—a distinction which is found in the color of the two races, and which must always exist so long as white men are distinguished from the other races by color—has no tendency to destroy the legal equality of the two races. The object of the Fourteenth Amendment was undoubtedly to enforce the absolute equality of the two races before the law, but in the nature of things it could not have been intended to abolish distinctions based upon color, or to enforce social, as distinguished from political equality, or a commingling of the races terms unsatisfactory to either.

The Plessy decision set the precedent that "separate" facilities for blacks and whites were constitutional as long as they were "equal," and this doctrine was quickly extended to cover many areas of public life. Not until 1954, in the equally important *Brown versus Board of Education* decision, would the "separate but equal" doctrine be struck down.

By 1890, most of the South, including Atlanta, was under the white rule. The first laws to take away Negro rights came as early as 1870, but most Jim Crow laws came in the following 25 years. Jim Crow laws required that whites and blacks use separate public facilities.

Reformers thought reducing contact between whites and blacks would thereby reduce the potential for racial violence. The term "Jim Crow" referred to a black character in a popular song composed in the 1830s. These laws were first developed in a few Northern states in the late 1800s, and then spread to the Southern states. One of the firm supporters of Jim Crow laws was the Klu Klux Klan, and the Jim Crow opponents were the Knights of Labor.

From 1890 to 1910, each Southern state wrote into their constitution laws that kept blacks from enjoying the privileges and rights of white men and women. During the era of Jim Crow, blacks were degraded in magazines, newspapers, nursery rhymes, popular songs, cartoons, movies, and jokes. "Jim Crow" was pictured as childlike, humorous, stupid, and dangerous. In Oklahoma, telephone booths were segregated. Mississippi had separate soft-drink machines for blacks and whites. In Atlanta, an African American could not "swear to tell the truth" on the same Bible used by white witnesses. In North Carolina, factories were separated into black and white sections. In some Alabama towns, it was against the law for blacks and whites to play cards, checkers, dominoes, or other games together. In Florida, school textbooks for white and black students were segregated in separate warehouses. In Washington, D.C., blacks could not bury their dead dogs or cats in the same pet cemeteries used by whites. Public parks were segregated. Even jails and prisons had separate sections for black prisoners. One law tried to stop black and white cotton-mill workers from looking out the same window! In Mobile, AL, blacks had to be off the streets by ten o' clock each evening. White taxi drivers could not carry black passengers. Black drivers could not accept white passengers. There were Jim Crow elevators in office buildings. A black child could not buy an ice-cream cone at a white stand. Black college professors—and any other black Americans—could not use a public library. There were separate hospitals for the two races. White nurses could not treat black men. Even if a black man was dying, he would not be admitted to a "white" hospital.

Some states had separate prisons. If an African American wanted to attend a theater or a movie, he had to buy his ticket at a separate booth. He had to enter by a separate entrance. He had to sit in the balcony, well apart from any white people. A black person was kept apart from white people all of his or her life, and then, when he died, he had to be buried by a black funeral home in a black cemetery. This was Jim Crow from birth to death. Jim Crow was the way of life; its touch soiled each day of a negro's life.

Because of the separate standards in the practice of medicine, African-American doctors meeting in Atlanta organized themselves at the First Congregational Church and established the National Medical Association. By the early 1900s, there were numerous African-American doctors in Atlanta.

Education for African-American children in Atlanta was totally segregated. Students attended private schools such as the Fourth Ward, Summerhill, and Gate City Schools from the turn of the 20th century to the 1960s.

In 1899, Dr. W.E.B. DuBois and others protested the 1899 statute segregating sleeping cars on trains. For public transportation in Atlanta, streetcars were used though they were segregated. African Americans had to enter from the rear. Professor George A. Towns of Atlanta University boycotted streetcars and rode his bicycle to work.

President William H. Taft visited the First Congregational Church (above) and the Big Bethel AME Church. Bishop Wesley J. Gaines presided over the program, and the Atlanta Glee Club sang "The Star Spangled Banner."

16

Two
THE ATLANTA BRANCH OF THE **NAACP**

On February 9, 1909, on the 100th anniversary of Abraham Lincoln's birthday, 60 prominent black and white citizens issued "The Call" for a national conference in New York City to renew "the struggle for civil and political liberty." A distinguished group of black leaders added their voice to the movement. Principal among these was W.E.B. Dubois, who was to serve as the sage of black professionals to form the Niagara Movement, which drew up an agenda for aggressive action. Also involved was Ida Well Barnett, a young journalist, whose eloquent editorials focused national attention on the epidemic of lynchings. Participants at the conference agreed to work towards the abolition of forced segregation, the promotion of equal education and civil rights under the protection of law, and an end to race violence. In 1911, that organization was incorporated as the National Association for the Advancement of Colored People, the NAACP.

The distinctive strategic emphasis of the NAACP, ending discrimination through legal action, evolved during its first 20 years. By assuming the legal challenges that were required to gain full citizenship for blacks, the association became a formidable force for change even in its early years. In 1910, in *Guinn versus United States*, the Supreme Court struck down the grandfather clauses of state constitutions as an unconstitutional barrier to voting rights under the 15th Amendment. In 1917, the Supreme Court declared unconstitutional a Louisville ordinance that required blacks to live in certain sections of the city, thus challenging residential segregation through city ordinances. The court decision to follow, initiated through NAACP lawsuits, nullified the restrictive covenants, a clause in real estate deeds that pledged a white buyer never to sell the property to blacks. And in 1923, the court declared that exclusion of blacks from a jury was inconsistent with the right to a fair trial. Thus, in just a few years, formidable obstacles to black voting, integrated communities, and integrated juries had been removed through concerted legal action. The NAACP then widened its scope and faced the next barrier to equal rights. Case precedents were established. The process was slow and evolutionary, but as history has demonstrated, it was the only way to win full constitutional guarantees for the rights of minorities.

In 1919, to awaken the national conscience, the NAACP published an exhaustive review of lynching records entitled, *Thirty Years of Lynching in the United States, 1889–1918*. NAACP leaders, with potential risk to their own lives, conducted first-hand investigations of racially motivated violence.

Though bills succeeded in passing the House of Representatives several times, they were always defeated in the Senate. Nonetheless, NAACP efforts brought an end to the excesses of mob violence through public exposure and the public pressure it mobilized.

The Atlanta branch of the NAACP was organized in 1917 and has remained a viable organization serving the needs of its constituents.

Members of the executive board of the Atlanta branch of the NAACP pose for a photograph. Professor Charles Lincoln Harper (center) was president, *c.* 1951.

18

The founders of the Atlanta branch of the NAACP were Harry Pace, Dr. Charles Johnson, Dr. Louis T. Wright, Walter F. White, Peyton Allen, George Alexander Towns, Benjamin Davis Sr., Rev. L.H. King, Dr. William F. Penn, John Hope, David H. Sims, William S. Cannon, and W.T. Cunningham. Pictured above is NAACP founder W.E.B. DuBois and Atlanta chapter founder John Hope.

In 1917, Harry Pace served as first president of the Atlanta branch of the NAACP. He was a former insurance executive and owned the Black Swan record company.

Rev. R.A. Singleton, the second president of the Atlanta branch, also served as pastor of the Big Bethel A.M.E. Church on Auburn Avenue.

In the 1920s, Rev. Adam Daniel Williams served as the third president of the Atlanta branch. He was the second pastor of Ebenezer Baptist Church, and married Jennie Celeste Williams. They were the parents of one daughter, Alberta. Alberta married Rev. Martin Luther King, Sr., and gave birth to Martin Luther King, Jr., in 1929 in the very home where the many of the early meetings of the Atlanta chapter were held.

The fourth president of the Atlanta branch was attorney Austin T. Walden. Attorney Walden was one of the most outspoken advocates of civil rights in Atlanta.

Forrester B. Washington, head of the Atlanta University School of Social Work, served as the fifth president of the Atlanta branch of the NAACP.

E. Luther Brooks was a distinguished educator at Clark College. He was elected as the sixth president of the Atlanta branch.

T.M. Alexander was the Atlanta branch's seventh president. In 1957, he campaigned for the Seventh Ward alderman seat. It was the first time in 87 years that an African American had attempted to be elected to the Board of Aldermen in Atlanta. A 1931 graduate of Morehouse College, Alexander was the founder and president of the Alexander Company and General Agency and vice president of the Alexander-Calloway Realty Company and the Southeastern Fidelity Fire Insurance Company, which he began in 1950. For many years, he served as a director for the Mutual Federal Savings and Loan Company.

Bishop William Wilkes (then a minister) was elected as the eighth president of the Atlanta branch. He was the pastor of numerous AME churches before being elected to the episcopacy as bishop.

In 1924, Charles Lincoln Harper, a graduate of Morris Brown College, was named as the first principal of Atlanta's first public high school for African-American children. Professor Harper had a brilliant tenure as the ninth president of the Atlanta branch. He was also very active in securing rights for Atlanta teachers, serving as the executive secretary of the Georgia Teachers Education Association. He died in 1955.

John H. Calhoun was born in Greenville, SC. A members of the Hampton Institute and Morehouse College Class of 1937, Calhoun became the first African American hired by the U.S. Veterans Hospital in Tuskegee, AL. Even though he was threatened by the Klu Klux Klan, he remained in that post for seven years. One of the co-founders of the Atlanta Negro Voters League, Calhoun served as the tenth president of the Atlanta branch of the NAACP as well as serving on the Atlanta City Council.

Rev. Harold I. Bearden, the 11th president of the Atlanta branch, was also elected bishop of the AME Church.

Dr. Samuel Williams, pastor of
Friendship Baptist Church, was an
outstanding advocate for civil rights
causes in Atlanta and was the president
of the Atlanta Branch of the NAACP
when the Atlanta University Center
Student protest was initiated. Williams
along with other leaders met with
Mayor Hartsfield to demand the release
of the students from the city jail.

In 1956, NAACP Regional Director
Ruby Hurley moved the regional
office to the Waluhaje Apartments
on West Lake Street. Thirty cases of
stationery were shipped to the
Cannonlene Building on Hunter
Street. By this time, the Georgia
Bureau of Investigation had begun
an investigation into the activities of
the NAACP.

The executive committee of the NAACP is pictured *c.* 1960 following a dinner at the Waluhaje. They are as follows: (standing) Rev. Samuel Williams (president, Atlanta branch), Mrs. Ruth Sturdivant, attorney A.T. Walden (attorney for the Atlanta branch), Isabel Webster (attorney for Atlanta branch), and Alfred Baker Lewis (national treasurer); (seated) Rev. Amos Holmes (Georgia field director), Mrs. Alfred Baker Lewis, Eunice Cooper (secretary, Atlanta branch), and Mrs. Amos Holmes.

Dr. C. Miles Smith, a graduate of Morehouse College, was named the 13th president of the Atlanta branch. He was succeeded by Dr. Albert M. Davis (pictured), one of Atlanta's most respected physicians.

The next presidents were Lonnie King, J.W. Couch, and Julian Bond (above left), who was elected as the 18th president of the Atlanta branch. (See p. 118 for more on Mr. Bond.) Other presidents that would follow included Dr. Otis Smith, elected as the 19th president of the Atlanta Branch of the NAACP. A graduate of Morehouse College, Otis Smith was a well-known Atlanta physician. Dr. Robert Threatt (above right), former president of Morris Brown College, was elected as the 20th president of the Atlanta branch. The current president is Rev. R.L. White, pastor of the Mount Ephraim Baptist Church.

Rev. Martin Luther King, Sr., led one of the first voter registration marches in Atlanta in 1935. They are pictured passing Ebenezer Baptist Church, on the corner of Auburn Avenue and Jackson Street, headed to city hall. As they began the march, Rev. King explained to all participating what kind of behavior was expected. More than a 1,000 people had gathered for the rally. Dr. King remarked the following to the overwhelming crowd: "I know one thing, I ain't gonna plow no more mules. I'll never step off the road again to let white folks pass. I am going to move forword toward freedom, and I'm hoping everybody here today is going right along with me!" It was the first time that many citizens had seen such a demonstration as the people marched in straight, orderly rows.

In 1949, African Americans participated in the first city primary and elected William B. Hartsfield, who remained in office until 1961.

These photographs were taken from the Mitchell Street side of the courthouse showing the massive line of black Atlantans waiting to register to vote in the primary of 1944.

Jondelle Harris Johnson, a former journalist for the *Atlanta Inquirer* and the *Atlanta Voice* newspapers, used the pen to express her disdain against police brutality, segregation at the city prison farm, and discrimination in the postal system. A former teacher and principal in the Atlanta, Cobb, and DeKalb Public School systems, Jondelle took the helm of the Atlanta branch of the NAACP in 1972. During her tenure, the Atlanta branch filed landmark lawsuit against Cox Enterprises that resulted in bringing African-American personalities and executives to corporate positions. She helped to create one of the most active and viable branches in the country. She died on March 30, 1998, and her successor, Judith Withers Hanson, has taken the helm of the premier civil rights organization in Atlanta.

Rev. J.A. Dorsey shakes hands with Mayor William Hartsfield during a gathering of African-American Baptist preachers, *c.* 1950.

(Paid Political Advertisement)
(Paid Political Advertisement)
THE ATLANTA
NEGRO VOTERS LEAGUE
Appeals To
All Registered Voters
Go To The Polls
Wed., Dec. 4th
The Atlanta Negro Voters League
Endorses All Nominees In Primary
Election Held May 8th, 1957
By Pulling One Lever In The Voting
Machine, You Will Vote For All The
Nominees Who Won In The May 8th
Primary, Including
Mayor
Wm. B. Hartsfield
It Will Take You Less Than A

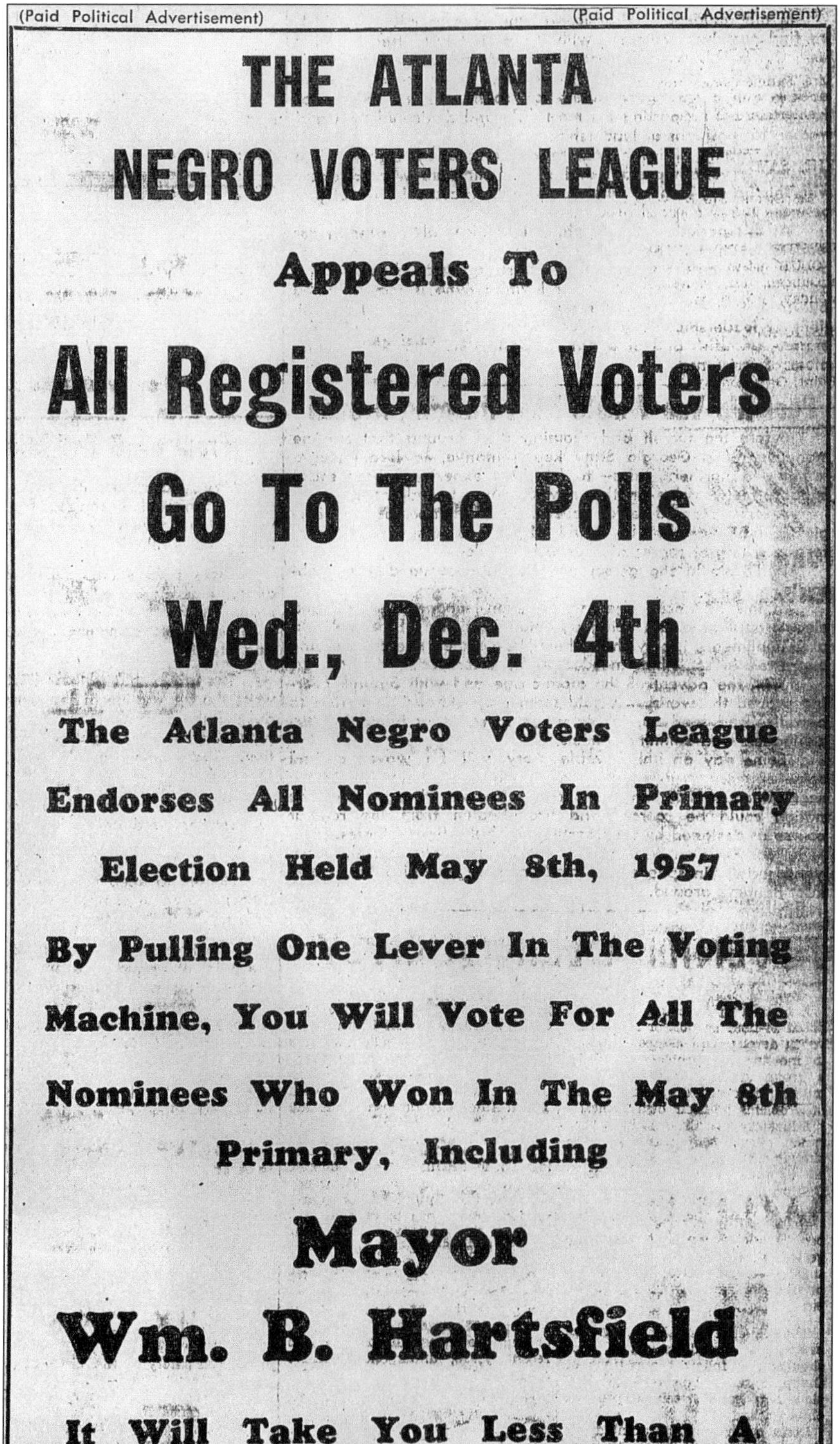

The Atlanta Negro Voters League urged African-American citizens to vote in the 1957 election.

Three
THE POWER OF
THE BALLOT: 1940S

" 'Lawd, they marchin again,' I heard more than one person lining the way
call out. And I yelled back a dozen ore more times, every few blocks:
'yes, and you come on 'n march with us, brother; walk with us, sister...' "

—Rev. Martin Luther King, Sr., *c.* 1935

African Americans in Atlanta were unable to utilize the public library. W.E.B. DuBois led a delegation into the newly dedicated Carnegie Library in 1902 and asked library trustees to open the building to all people, arguing that public libraries should benefit both races. DuBois cited the illegality of using tax money to support library facilities for whites only. The trustee promised a separate library for African Americans. Nineteen years later, in 1921, the Auburn Branch (pictured) opened, with Mrs. Alice Dugged Carey as the first librarian.

IMPORTANT MEETING!
ATLANTA CIVIC - POLITICAL LEAGUE
Will Meet at Ebenezer Baptist Church
REV. M. L. KING, Pastor

TUESDAY NIGHT, AUG. 5, 1941; 8:30 O'CLOCK
All Interested Negro Citizens Are Invited to Attend

John Wesley Dobbs, Pres.   Joseph Crawford, Sec'y

Here is an announcement of the Atlanta Civic and Political League from 1941. On Abraham Lincoln's birthday, in February 1936, the Civic and Political League was established with John Wesley Dobbs as president and Joseph Crawford as secretary. Meetings were held throughout the city at local churches, giving the African-American voters an opportunity to hear candidates. With its creation, they were able to double the vote of African Americans by the next election in 1944.

Register NOW

WHY? In order to help get more and better schools, streets and lights, and police protection. **REGISTRATION DOES NOT COST A PENNY!** It is the duty of every citizen to **REGISTER AND VOTE.**

HOW? You will be asked the following questions: Name? Address? Age? (Anyone 18 years or over may register.) Mother's name before marriage (maiden name)? Type of work (occupation)? How long have you lived in Atlanta?

WHERE? If you live in DeKalb County, go to: The DeKalb County Courthouse in Decatur, Georgia. If you live in Fulton County go to: The Fulton County Courthouse in Atlanta, Georgia.

YOU WILL RECEIVE COURTEOUS TREATMENT FROM THE REGISTRAR.

WHEN? NOW. Monday thru Friday, 9 A.M. to 5:00 P.M. Saturdays, 9 A.M. to 12 Noon.

REGISTER YOURSELF! Take Another To Register!

EVERY CITIZEN A QUALIFIED VOTER

Pictured is an announcement of the Citizens Democratic Club of Fulton County. In 1944, C.A. Scott, editor of the *Atlanta Daily World*, attorney A.T. Walden, and others formed the Citizens Democrat Club. It was billed as the official "Negro" Democratic Organization in the country. The officers were President C.A. Scott, Vice President Dr. R.A. Billings, Treasurer J.A. Batts, Assistant Secretary Charles W. "Pete" Greenlea, and counsel attorney A.T. Walden.

Rev. Martin Luther King, Sr., was a vocal civil rights activist long before his son was in the 1950s. King publicly demonstrated the hiring of African-American policemen in the 1940s.

African Americans line up around the Fulton County Courthouse to register to vote, many for the first time, 1946.

The designated "colored" entrance into the courthouse is seen as potential registrants line up and wait patiently to enter, 1946.

From Pryor Street to Mitchell Street to Hunter Street, African Americans in Atlanta were in lines that literally wrapped around the buildings and businesses, *c.* 1944.

One of the unsung heroes of the Atlanta branch of the NAACP was Virgil Wendell Hodges. Hodges, who worked as the chairman of the Sociology Department at Clark College and was dean at Albany State, moved to Atlanta in 1935 and joined the Atlanta branch. Hodges, along with historian C.A. Bacote, Eugene Martin, and A.T. Walden, attempted to test the refusal of whites to allow blacks to vote in the primary elections of 1944. The men drove to the all-white precinct on Bankhead but were denied because their name did not appear on a list. It created a flurry of action within the branch. In 1983, Hodges was honored by the Atlanta branch for the acquiring the largest amount of new members in a single year. Ironically, hours before his death, he solicited 20 names for membership.

William "Pete" Greenlea speaks at a voter registration rally at Wheat Street Baptist Church, *c.* the 1940s. The effort to motivate African-American citizens to register created a sense of pride and awareness in the community. Powerful oration, preaching, and music stirred the crowds.

The line to vote at the precinct at E.R. Carter on Ashby Street wrapped completely around the building, *c.* 1944. It was at this precinct that a white woman, Helen Douglass Mankin, received enough votes from African Americans to be elected to Congress from the 5th District of Georgia. Gov. Eugene Talmedge referred to Mankin as the "Belle of Ashby Street."

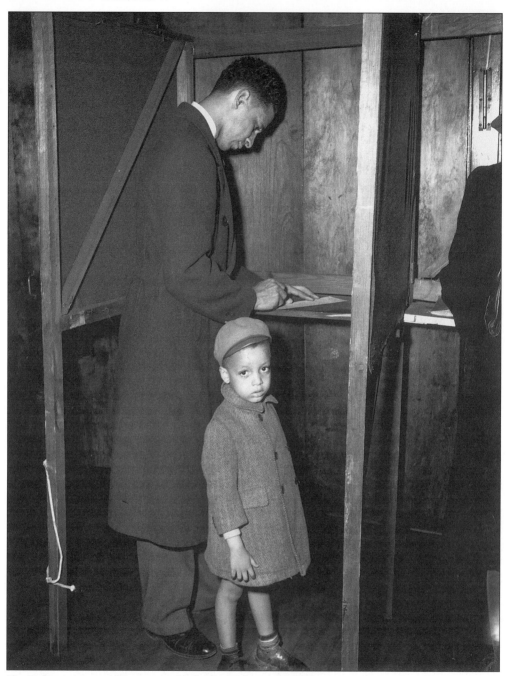

Mr. Nelson votes as his son stands by his side, *c*. the 1940s.

Four
THE ATLANTA EIGHT

"Never have used them here to do such work, and in my opinion we never will."
—J.L. Beamon, Atlanta chief of police, 1920

*"You are more than just policemen.
You are going out as the first representative of your race in Atlanta."*
—Mayor William B. Hartsfield, 1948

Officer Claude Dixon (standing) confers with fellow officer Ernest Lyons (seated) in Police Car No. 333, *c.* 1950s. By 1962, the city of Atlanta named its first African-American police lieutenant and removed the restriction prohibiting African-American officers from arresting white offenders and suspects. Detective Sgt. Howard Baugh, who joined the force in 1956, was named lieutenant and put in charge of an all-colored patrol division. Assisting him was Sgt. C.J. Perry. In making the promotions and announcing the changes, Police Chief Herbert Jenkins stated, "You cannot assign a man to guard against burglars and then tell him he can arrest a colored burglar, but not a white one." Baugh would be later promoted to captain, becoming, once again, the first African-American officer to receive such honors. Sgt. Robert McKibbens worked for the police bureau for 32 years.

As early as 1920, there were attempts to integrate the Atlanta Police Department. Distinguished physician Dr. Henry R. Butler asked the question in the *Atlanta Independent* newspaper, "Why Not Colored Police For the City of Atlanta?" J.L. Beamon, chief of police, declared that he has no colored men connected with the department. There were African-American officers in Washington, D.C., Baltimore, Boston, Philadelphia, New York, Chicago, Cleveland, and Pittsburgh but not in Atlanta.

Mayor Hartsfield had told the black leadership of Atlanta that if they were successful in registering 10,000 voters, he would work to get African-American policemen. *Newsweek* magazine had reported that 25 percent of the white Atlanta policemen were members of the Klu Klux Klan.

In December of 1947, white and black citizens crowded the Recorders Court in standing room capacity to hear arguments, pro and con, relative to the employment of African-American police. Boos and cat calls greeted the first few citizens who spoke in behalf of their measure. Also speaking at the program were C.A. Scott, general manager of the *Atlanta Daily World*, and Lorimer D. Milton, president of Citizens Trust Company.

That same month the city council okayed the resolution by Commissioner Ralph T. Huie calling for the employment of eight "Negro" officers to patrol negro communities. Immediately following the council's actions, a suit was filed by a local white undertaker, G. Herbert Yarn, to restrain the city from carrying out the action. Subsequently, the suit was dismissed by Superior Court Judge Bond Almand on the grounds that the enacted legislation had caused no harm. Professor Charles Lincoln Harper chaired the Negro Police Committee.

The Fulton County Grand Jury approved the hiring of the policemen, citing that the action was a step forward in law enforcement among the "Negro" race and should result in more respect of the law in Atlanta and Georgia. All departments of the city and county and various civic groups and individuals were asked to aid in seeing that the new policemen experiment was given a fair trial.

Advertisements for police jobs appeared in the *Atlanta Daily World* newspaper, with a deadline for application to close on Saturday, February 28, 1948. The applications were made available at the second floor of the city hall in the City Personnel Office. The age limits for police patrolmen was 21 to 35, with starting salary including a cost of living bonus at $203 a month. Over 100 applications were received. The initial examinations were taken at Smith Hughes High School on Pryor Street. Of the first 57 men who took the initial examination, only 13 qualified. This figure was later reduced to 2 when 11 of them failed to meet the physical address. Of the last 40 applicants, 6 qualified. Many of them were disqualified due to poor eyesight and being overweight. Of the 8 men who were chosen, 6 had been to college and 7 fought in World War II. The officers were paid $196 a month and worked 6 days a week. Several examinations would be necessary for the 8, including a mental aptitude and medical examination. Donned in their trunks and sneakers, the men were put through a battery of tests including rope climbing, chinning, and cat walking. The 8 men's last exam was an oral exam, which sought biographical data for the City Personnel Department. Its purpose was to assure that each applicant possessed no traits of "moral turpitude." The officers selected included Johnnie P. Jones, 29; Williard Strickland, 25; John Sanders Jr., 26; Willie T. Elkins, 33; Robert McKibbens, 26; Henry Hudson Hooks, 31; Ernest H. Lyons, 28; and Claude Dixon II, 21.

John H. Sanders, one of the 8 selected, had been salutatorian of his class at Booker T. Washington in 1942 and was employed as a janitor at Clark Howell School.

The prospective officers began a rigorous 8 weeks of training under the supervision of Capt. C.D. Hardeman and Lt. E.S. Elliot. They had to report everyday at 8 a.m. until the training was completed, bringing with them gym clothing. Their training program had been endorsed by the Federal Bureau of Investigation, the State Board of Education, and the Veterans Training Service. It was identical to what the white officers in the department had received. It was a rainy Monday morning in March of 1948, when 8 African Americans were sworn in by a Chief Herbert Jenkins. In his remarks to them, he exhorted that they must be on their toes at all time and for them to feel free to call him at any time. He said, "It'll take time for the citizens both white and colored to get used to you for you will be a novelty." They were also warned against graft, bribery, brutality, and other inducements that might present themselves.

The police department had identified a section of a two-story building that housed a pool hall and confectionary at Ellis and Butler Street which would be leased and used as the the precinct for the African-American officers. The owner, Steve Arthur, would lease it for $1 a year. The city would use the Butler Street YMCA as the temporary precinct for the officers.

On the very first day, Mayor Hartsfield and Chief Herbert Jenkins came down to the Butler Street YMCA and talked to the officers. He told them: "Now, you young men are wearing the same uniform as white officers, carrying the same equipment, getting the same pay. You are policemen. You are policemen! You cannot arrest white people. But if you see an old white drunk coming down your beat, bouncing off the building, just go the call box and have him picked up. We'll lock him up." Officer Henry Hooks recalled Jenkins saying, "Ninety five percent of the white officers don't want you, so you are going to be on trial, and you are going to have to show them you can police just as well as they can." The officers were under the command of a white sergeant.

When they came out of the YMCA and began to make their rounds on their first beat on Auburn Avenue vicinity on April 3, 1948, Ernest Lyons recalled that there were hundreds of citizens in front of the Y, many of whom would eventually follow them around. Their first arrest was made on the corner at Ellis and Butler Street at a wine store where a man and woman were fighting.

Officer Willie Elkins served only two months. He was discontented with the restraints and restrictions placed on them. Officer John Sanders left the police force within a year and reenlisted in the Army. Willard Stricken had the distinction of becoming the first African-American police officer for Decatur, GA, in 1964. Officer Johnnie Jones organized the Precinct Club for the original members to talk and discuss ideas.

The first black Atlanta police officer killed in the line of duty was Claude Mundy, in 1961. When Mundy reached the door at a potential crime site, the suspect was wielding a small .22-caliber pistol. Mundy did not see the gun and was shot.

Seated in their first official photograph are the following officers: (standing) Henry Hooks, Claude Dixon, and Ernest Lyons; (standing) Robert McKibbens, Williard Strickland, Willie T. Elkins, Johnnie P. Jones, and John Sanders.

On a Friday in April 1948, an overflow crowd of several thousand citizens turned out to Greater Mt. Calvary Baptist Church, which was pastored by Rev. B.J. Johnson, to witness the public induction service of the 8 police officers by the Atlanta branch of the NAACP. Mayor William B. Hartsfield was the keynote speaker and Chief of Police Herbert Jenkins introduced the officers. Officer Willie T. Elkins represented the policemen. He remarked that he considered the appointment a challenge and an opportunity that would be met and carried through to success. In September of 1948, the Fulton County Grand Jury praised the service of the policemen. The following month, the first case presented by an African-American officer in the criminal court occurred when Officers Johnnie Jones and Henry Hooks brought charges against John Henry Williams for handling illegal whiskey. The judge found Williams guilty and ordered that he be fined $300 or serve 12 months on the county public works. The officers testified that Williams was found possessing 40 gallons of non-taxed whiskey.

By October of 1949, 18 months after the arrival of Atlanta's first African-American police, these men began rotating assignments in two newly purchased police cars, which were operated by the African-American police from 5 p.m. to 1 a.m. every day, except Sunday. Car number 13 patrolled the territory that included North Avenue and Piedmont, the Georgia and Southern Railroad belt line, Highland Avenue, Parkway Drive, Pine Street, and Hunt Street, while car number 21 covered Simpson Street at the city limits to Ashby Streets, to North Avenue to Magnolia Street, to Elliot Street to Nelson Street, to Walker Street, to Peters Street to Leonard Street, to West End Avenue, to Ashby Street to West View Drive to the railroad, and to the city limits.

Three made it to retirement. Hooks, McKibbens and Lyons retired in 1980. Tragically, Dixon committed suicide in 1982.

In 1965, Officers George Burnett and Gus Thornhill, Jr., became the first African-American police officers in East Point, GA, a town on the outskirts of Atlanta.

Known as the "Superchief," A. Reginald Eaves, a native of Jacksonville, FL, and a graduate of Morehouse, became chief of police in 1974 following a stint as the commissioner of the Boston penal system. In 1973, Eaves served as one of the advisors to Maynard Jackson's mayoral campaign. While a student at Morehouse in 1955, Eaves participated in a boycott of Atlanta's segregated bus system. Police Chief Eaves served until 1978.

Lee P. Brown (right) was elected public safety commissioner and George Napper, a graduate of the School of Criminology at the University of California at Berkeley, was named chief of police following Eaves resignation in 1978.

Zep Gel

Lubie Geter
MISSING CHILD

Eldrin Bell worked his way up through the ranks of the Atlanta Police Department before he became chief of police. A graduate of David T. Howard High School, Bell attended Morris Brown College before joining the police department. Bell, like his predecessors, were all mindful of the path blazed by the first African-American policemen "the Atlanta Eight."

In 1994, Major Beverly J. Harvard, a native of Macon, GA, and a graduate of Morris Brown College, became the first African-American woman elected as the chief of a major police department in the country.

Five

RUBY BLACKBURN, NOW THAT WAS A WOMAN!

Mrs. Ruby Blackburn was the founder of the Georgia League of Negro Women voters. A beautician by profession, she attended Morris Brown College and graduated from Apex College. She established the Royal Nine Social Club and later the TIC (To Improve Conditions club), where she was successful in placing African-American clerks in chain stores. Through her tireless efforts, she was able to secure a school in the Dixie Hills area known as the Pine Acres School and the Davis Street School. Her major emphasis was on the Atlanta Cultural League Training Center located at 229 Auburn Avenue.

One of the primary goals of the league was that every woman and girl of legal age be registered as as voter. Educational classes were taught about what candidates stood for and their ability to serve all of the people. The other goals of the league included examining civil problems and community services, such as safety programs including lights, crosswalks, policewomen where needed, sewer conditions, slum clearances, street and sidewalk improvements, and tax eliminations. In 1957, African-American women took on the Georgia Legislature. Members of the League of Negro Women Voters visited the 1957 session of the Georgia Legislature. Mrs. J.B. Blayton, director of the Blayton School of Accounting, was education chairman for the League of Negro Women Voters.

Mrs. Ruby Blackburn demonstrates the voting machine. Shown are Mrs. Frances Fouch, Mrs. Sadie Powell, and Mrs. Odessa Davis, principal of Alonzo F. Herndon School, *c.* 1959.

Mrs. Blackburn swears in poll workers at the E.R. Carter Elementary School, *c.* 1950s. From left to right are Mrs. Annie Turner, Mrs. Eunice Cooper, Mrs. Marjorie Fowlkes, Mrs. John Taylor, Mrs. Ruby Blackburn, Mrs. W.E. Lloyd, Q.V. Williamson, Mrs. Vashti Ellis, Mrs. Sadie Whitehead, and Mrs. Hattie Holmes.

A poll worker checks for names on the eligible voting list, *c.* 1960s.

Residents exercise their right to vote, *c.* 1960.

Here, citizens are voting at the E.R. Carter Elementary School. Mr. Hayden Whitney, manager of the poll, stands in the center as an Atlanta police officer gets ready to vote.

Six

THE GATE CITY BAR ASSOCIATION

"As to the role and responsibility of the Negro lawyer in the future, we must not for a moment credulously believe or think that the walls of all Jericho have been leveled; that all the Rubicund have crossed, nor that we have possessed the promised land."

—Attorney Austin T. Walden
Speech at the Hungry Club Forum, *c.* 1959

William Reeves (left) and Samuel Davis (right) were plaintiffs in the law suit for equalization of teachers' salaries. Reeves filed the suit, and Davis replaced him as plaintiff. Senator Herman Talmedge claimed at a GTEA convention that he equalized salaries during his administration, a statement with which Reeves vehemently disagreed.

There are a number of facets that have contributed to the success of Atlanta's racial climate. While many will argue that there is still much work to be done, the efforts of Atlanta's African-American lawyers, from the 1800s to the founding of the Gate City Bar Association (GCBA) in 1948, and now almost 50 years later, is, as they sang in some African-American churches, "worthy to be praised."

The first known African-American lawyer in Atlanta was William A. Pledger, who lived in Atlanta in the 1880s. Attorney Pledger was one of the most important political leaders in Georgia during the 19th century. Born to a slave mother and a white father near Jonesboro in 1852, he attended Atlanta University and taught school in Athens in the 1870s. When the Democrats closed his school in Athens in 1872, Pledger, a staunch Republican, stumped the state for the Republican party and was a delegate to every Republican national convention from 1876 to 1900. Pledger also founded several newspapers in Atlanta, the *Weekly, Defiance,* the *Reporter,* and the *Age.* He was very militant in demanding more rights for blacks. President Chester A. Arthur appointed Pledger surveyor of customs in Atlanta. He opened a practice with Thomas Malone. A few years before his death, Pledger testified before a Congressional committee in 1902 on lynchings and made the following remark: "Men have been lynched simply that their crops might revert to the landlord." So active was his fight that he once led armed blacks to the Athens jail and successfully defied a mob bent on lynching two prisoners. He was a fearless, outspoken advocate of justice until his death in 1904.

Pledger was followed by a succession of men including Charles H.J. Taylor, Henry Lincoln Johnson, and Peyton Allen (pictured above). Men who were prohibited from attending law schools but were allowed to apprentice in the law offices of white lawyers were granted the privilege to "read law." This process engaged them in reading and gaining knowledge of the laws and statutes of the state of Georgia. They were referred to as "colonel," a title bestowed upon them that gave them some respectability in their community, but which saved whites from having to call them "mister."

The 1912 Atlanta Negro Directory, a source that preceded the Atlanta Black Pages by 75 years, listed three lawyers, Peyton Allen, P.A Chappelle, and Henry Lincoln Johnson, whose separate offices were located on Broad Street.

Henry "Linc" Johnson was well respected by the Atlanta Bar. It was no surprise when Matt Waterloo Bullock, a graduate of Harvard University, approached Johnson and encouraged him to help him get admitted to the Georgia Bar without taking the exam. Johnson was successful in this maneuver, and Bullock opened a practice on Broad Street. Col. Henry Lincoln Johnson, a native of Augusta, GA, was a graduate of Atlanta University and the University of Michigan, where he received his law degree. In 1913, he began practicing law at his office at 16 1/2 North Broad Street. He was the attorney for the Atlanta Life Insurance

Company and, later, the recorder of deeds for the District of Columbia. Johnson was an outspoken advocate for political rights and used his oratorical abilities to expose petty politics, discrimination, and segregation in government service. A staunch republican and an Odd Fellow, he married Georgia Douglass, a distinguished Harlem Renaissance poet and a Atlanta University graduate. They were the parents of one son, Peter. In 1922, Attorney Johnson represented, in the Supreme Court of the District of Columbia, Algenon Simpkins, a young black male who had been charged with criminally assaulted a white girl under 16 years of age. Johnson was an intimate acquaintance and personal friend of the defendant's family, who had lived in Georgia. Following Johnson's display of eloquence and forceful argument, the all-white jury, after six hours, reported to the court that they were in "hopeless disagreement."

The Standard Life Insurance Company gave him a job as their legal adviser for $25 per month. He later found employment as the legal counselor for the Odd Fellows organization at $440 a year. Bullock left Atlanta, after an unsuccessful stint as a lawyer, to teach at Alabama A&M in Normal, AL.

By 1919, Estelle A. Henderson, a member of the faculty at Morris Brown College and a lawyer who had already been admitted to the bar in Alabama, had acquired office space in the Odd Fellows building on Auburn Avenue. She was informed that after having completed the formalities to practice in Georgia, she would be admitted to the Georgia Bar. No record exists of her having been actually admitted or practicing in Atlanta.

J.E. Sistrunk, though not a trained lawyer, may have best used the legal system to voice the despairing treatment of blacks, when in 1922 he filed, in the United State Supreme Court, a brief charging that "Negroes" in Georgia were being deprived of their legal rights in courts. Several cases were cited in his brief. Though his background offered some questionable activity, he was considered a nemesis to the all-white court system and was one of the most memorable African-American litigants during the 1920s in Atlanta. One newspaper source is quoted as saying "that if Sistrunk is admitted to the bar, he will prove that white men and women now hold millions of dollars worth of property . . . on residential and business sections . . . that of right belongs to Negroes."

Peyton Allen, also a graduate of Atlanta, had already established himself as an outspoken advocate of civil rights. Born in Blackshear, GA, in the 1800s, Colonel Allen was a successful educator who taught in Perry, GA, and later assumed the principalship of the Mitchell Street School in Atlanta. As an advocate for the uplift of his race, he served in the Georgia Suffrage League. In 1899, he was admitted to the Georgia Bar; however, he did not open his practice until 1906.

The decade of the 1920s was significant both nationally and locally for African-American lawyers. In 1925, a group of black lawyers organized the National Bar Association in Des Moine, IO, an organization that would unite and bring together black attorneys throughout the country. The organization began meeting annually in various cities to discuss issues affecting them. A.T. Walden, one of two black attorneys in Atlanta, became an active member.

In 1927, Walden, then Atlanta's lone black lawyer, won a decisive victory over the Atlanta Police Department when he convinced a white grand jury that a group of officers had overstepped their boundaries when they arrested Dr. C.A. Spence, a black dentist, on charges of disorderly conduct because he refused to leave a "Jim Crow" street car. A group of street car conductors had ordered every black off of the cars so that they could socialize and drink, according to the charges. When he and his wife refused to leave, he was beaten, taken into custody by the police, and charged.

Walden's ability to help young lawyers was unmatched. On October 24, 1930, he motioned the U.S. Supreme Court to admit John Geer, an Atlanta attorney, to practice before the court. It was believed to have been the first time that a black attorney had issued a motion on behalf of another.

With a law degree in hand from Harvard Law School, Benjamin Jefferson Davis, Jr., returned to his former home of Atlanta and set up a law practice. He had grown up in Atlanta with his father, the fiery newspaper paper publisher and editor of the *Atlanta Independent*. Ben Sr. chastised and called to task the white political structure of Atlanta. Like his father, Ben Jr. had a colorful career in Atlanta. During his first year as a lawyer, he offered his services to a young black man, Angelo Herndon, who had been charged with "insurrection" against the state of Georgia for having organized a demonstration of the unemployed of both races. The trial was, according to Davis, "a turning point in his life." Davis remarked, "the trial exposed the in all of its nakedness, the racist and class character of Southern justice." In 1933, Davis joined the Communist party, and two years later, he left Atlanta and went to New York City, where he became editor of the weekly newspaper *Negro Liberator*. He continued to aid in the defense of such cases as the Scottsboro boys, the Atlanta Six, and other cases of racist victimization and class injustice. He was elected to the New York City Council and was supported by luminaries such as Congressman Adam Clayton Powell and actress Lena Horne. Davis died on August 24, 1964, at the age of 60.

By the time the 1930s rolled around, many blacks had become concerned because of the lack of blacks passing the Georgia State Bar exam. One newspaper reported that it had been ten years since a black had passed the bar. Lawyers such as A.T. Walden and others were generally excluded from the activities of the State Bar Association, and by the late 1940s, a long overdue need—to create an organization that would address the special needs of black lawyers—was realized.

The decade of the 1930s was also dismal for African-American lawyers in Atlanta, in part due to the outcome of the Angelo Herndon case and the actions of Benjamin Jefferson Davis Jr. Many remarked that his actions following the trial had made it virtually impossible for blacks to have a fair chance to pass the state bar. The 1940s would bring about a change both locally and nationally with reference to blacks attempting to gain legal education and pass the bar. Attorney Walden, in his attempt to help black lawyers receive the respect and credibility they deserved, sent a letter to U.S. District Judge E. Marvin Underwood with a list of names of African-American lawyers in Atlanta who had passed the bar and who were available for representing indigent defendants. This opportunity would certainly give black attorneys more visibility and practice.

In 1948, the United States Supreme Court ruled in *Sipuel versus University of Oklahoma* that a state must provide legal education for blacks at the same time it is offered to whites. This ruling would prove to be significant, as the state of Georgia offered only two law schools, the University of Georgia and Emory University. Also, the GCBA was organized. Recently, the GCBA celebrated its anniversary and renewed its commitment to fulfill the original aims of the organization established 50 years ago by nine African-American attorneys who faced insurmountable odds. Their reasons for creating the organization were to "create in the community a practical appreciation for the legal profession; to encourage persons of outstanding promise to attend first rate law schools and the return to the communities which statistics demonstrated needed their services most; to be alert to oppose arbitrary and capricious laws in our state with all the force and fiber of which we are capable as an organization; to uphold and extend the principles of justices in every phase of American life to the end that no one shall be discriminated because of his color, race, religious beliefs or national origins."

The formation of the GCBA fostered the best and brightest legal minds in the city in 1948. For African Americans in Atlanta, racial and legal discrimination would show signs of victory as the city's first eight African-American police took to the streets of Atlanta in 1948. On the social front, black Atlantans patronized the infamous Top Hat Night Club, which, according to advertisements in the *Atlanta Daily World,* presented the "smartest" floor shows and dances. "Sweet" Auburn Avenue was experiencing its perennial "hey day," as black-owned businesses and black professionals flourished and prospered. It was the street where doctors, dentists, and lawyers opened their offices. On Butler Street, which was located off of Auburn, on January 25, 1948, at 5:25 p.m., nine African-American lawyers—Charles Morgan Clayton, Edward D'Antignac, Thomas J. Henry, Rachel Prudence Herndon, Thomas W. Holmes, Eugene E. Moore, Sylvester S. Robinson, and J.A. Salter—met in the office of attorney Austin T. Walden for the purpose of organizing "Negro lawyers in Atlanta."

Early minutes cite the discussion of the proposed name of the group. Two names were offered: the Gate City Bar Association and the Empire State Bar Association. The latter was selected, but after further discussion, attorney R.E. Thomas moved and Charles M. Clayton seconded that the vote on the name be rescinded and that the original motion naming the group the Gate City Bar Association be chosen. It was decided that any practicing retired lawyer in good standing would be admitted and out-of-city lawyers would be accepted as associate members. The first officers were A.T. Walden, president; Eugene E. Moore, vice president; Rachel P. Herndon, secretary; and R.E. Thomas, treasurer. The first constitution committee consisted of attorneys D'Antignac, Salter, Robinson, and Clayton. The meeting adjourned at 6:50, and thus, this group of black lawyers had given birth to an organization whose mission would be redefined over the years. Its founders were trailblazers in the law in Atlanta.

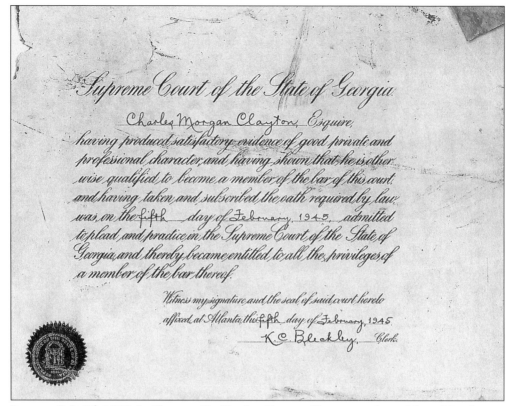

Born on July 26, 1888, in Clayton, AL, Charles Morgan Clayton graduated from Morehouse College in 1904 and received a master's in education from Atlanta University. He took law courses through LaSalle University's extension program in 1941, before obtaining his law degree in nine months from the John Marshall Law School in 1944. He also passed the bar the same year and practiced law under Attorney A.T. Walden. Above, the shingle of Charles Morgan Clayton, granting his jurisdiction to practice in the Supreme Court of State of Georgia, is pictured.

Though his law career came late in his life, Professor Clayton, as he was known, was a pioneer school teacher and principal at Bryant Preparatory School, a segregated high school on Auburn Avenue, from 1915 to 1932, where he taught Martin Luther King, Sr. He served as principal of the Herring Street School in Decatur from 1932 to 1952, when he decided to change careers and practice criminal law, which he did until 1982, the year he died.

Rachel Herndon was a product of the Atlanta public schools and a graduate of Atlanta University. Active in civic and community affairs, she began working with attorney A.T. Walden as his secretary in the 1930s. In 1937, she was the only black in a group of 80 people to take the law examination. Seven years later, on May 1, 1944, Rachel Pruden Herndon was admitted to practice law before the state supreme court. Attorney Herndon was instrumental in the establishment of the GCBA Women's Auxiliary Organization. She was active with the Atlanta branch of the NAACP. In 1956, she became the first African-American woman from Georgia to be admitted to practice before the U.S. Supreme Court. In December of 1965, Herndon was appointed by Mayor Ivan Allen as a pro-hoc judge for traffic and recorders court. She filled in the vacancy left by Judge A.T. Walden. Because of her work with the Democratic party of Georgia, she was invited to visit the White House, where she was personally greeted by Vice President Hubert Humphrey and President Lyndon B. Johnson. Judge Herndon's career as a judge was not always smooth. In 1973, she was brought before the city's board of ethics for her handling of cases involving organizations that she represented in her private law practice. She was exonerated from the charges and later retired from the bench and her practice. Judge R.P. Herndon died in January of 1979 and she was funeralized at Beulah Baptist Church, where she was a lifelong member. She is shown above in her courtroom.

Thomas W. Holmes was the oldest lawyer in Atlanta when the GCBA was founded. Born in Washington, GA, Attorney Holmes attended Atlanta University and later found employment as a mail carrier. It was during this time that he met attorney Peyton Allen and became an apprentice for him. It was in Allen's office where Holmes studied for two years before the he passed the state bar on June 12, 1912, and was granted the opportunity to practice. One of Holmes most publicized cases was the handling of the estate of the late Middleweight Boxing Champion "Tiger" Flowers, who died in 1927. Holmes was a member of the First Congregational Church. He married Mamie McKinley and had two daughters, Louise and Grace.

By 1954, Atlanta had become a fertile ground for African-American women attorneys, including Rachel Herndon, Cassandra Maxwell Burney, Romae L. Turner Powell, and Doris Blayton (pictured at right). Attorney Burney, a native of Orangeburg, SC, and a graduate of the Howard University Law School, became the first African-American woman in South Carolina to be admitted to the bar on November 3, 1938. Attorney Powell, a graduate of Spelman College and Howard University Law School, opened up her law practice in Atlanta in 1951, where she practiced until 1968, after which she served as referee and judge pro tempore. In 1973, she was named Fulton County Juvenile Justice, becoming the first African-American woman to be named a county judge. Attorney Blayton, a native of Atlanta, was admitted to the Georgia Bar in 1950, after graduating from Spelman College and the John Marshall Law School in 1949. Blayton's father, Jesse Blayton, was one of the first certified public accountants in the country. The Blayton family owned and operated WERD radio station, the nation's first black-owned and operated station, and the Blayton Business College, where Attorney Blayton served as president at one time. She also served as the head of the legal staff of the League of Negro Women Voters.

Perhaps the heart and soul of the Gate City Bar Association was Col. A.T. Walden, often referred to as the dean of black lawyers in Atlanta. Born on April 12, 1885, near Fort Valley, GA, Walden received his education at the public schools of Fort Valley and Atlanta University, where he graduated in 1907. He received his law degree from the University of Michigan in 1911. The following year, he returned to Macon, GA, to open a practice, which lasted until 1917, when he entered the Army and served as captain of Company I, 365th Infantry during World War I.

He was a life member of the National Bar Association and co-founder of the Atlanta Negro Voters League and became one of the first black delegates to the 1964 Democratic National Convention. His appointment as the alternate judge of the Municipal Courts of Atlanta was the first such appointment for a black person in the state of Georgia and the South, since the Reconstruction period. Walden died on July 2, 1965, at the age of 80.

Much activity took place in the legal realm after the *Brown versus Board of Education* decision in 1954. Black lawyers in Atlanta found themselves in demand, as many civil suits were being filed to obtain equal access to public accommodations. Though the number of black attorneys had increased during the 1950s, Atlanta still ranked far behind other cities.

In 1957, S.B. Wright, newly installed president of the GCBA, in his acceptance speech to the organization, predicted the following: "I am no prophet or fortune teller, neither am I the son of one. I can only prognosticate the future by the events of the past and present. I predict that we shall have not less than 299 layers of color in the City of Atlanta by the year 2000 A.D."

Two years after Wright's tenured, charter member R. Prudence Herndon was elected president and served until 1960. The close of the 1950s saw the admission of Leroy Johnson to the Georgia Bar Association in 1958 and to the GCBA.

The 1960s found black lawyers confronting many challenges, both professionally and personally. While some improvements had been made with regard to courthouse etiquette for black attorneys, the civil rights battleground was growing, and many black lawyers were deeply involved.

New members added to the association during the 1960s included Julius C. Daughtery, Isabel Gates Webster, and Horace Ward (pictured above). Ward, a graduate of Morehouse, had applied for admission to the University of Georgia Law School but was denied. He filed a suit in the federal district court. In 1957, after a seven-year struggle to gain entrance, Federal Judge Frank Hooper decided that the case was moot. Ward attended the Northwestern University School of Law and was admitted to the Georgia Bar in 1960. Isabel Gates Webster, a graduate of Boston University School of Law, had come from three generations of lawyers, including her great uncle and father. She participated in the defense of many employment discrimination cases, particularly *Sanders versus Dobbs House*. Julius C. Daughtery, a graduate of Clark College and the Howard University Law School, would go on to serve as a member of the Georgia House of Representatives in the 33rd House District and carve a distinguished career in law and politics.

As the heat of the Civil Rights Movement was turned up, so were cases involving attempts to gain constitutional rights. One of the leading attorneys was Donald Hollowell, who was president of the GCBA from 1960 to 1962. Hollowell was the chief counsel of the *Holmes/Hunter versus University of Georgia* case.

In what was considered a monumental step in race relations between black and white lawyers in Atlanta, nine Gate City lawyers attended a banquet of 1,300 white Atlanta lawyers, guests, and friends for Secretary of State Dean Rusk at the Atlanta Biltmore Hotel in April of 1961. The Gate City members were assured in a letter to then President Hollowell that they would be extended courteous treatment. This effort was a subtle step to began to open dialogue between black and white lawyers in Atlanta.

Since the 1950s, the GCBA has sponsored its National Bar Association Week with a series of programs and forums including hosting the popular Hungry Club Forum at the Butler Street YMCA. One of the primary efforts of the organization has always been to provide a public forum to discuss legal issues affecting African Americans.

Many of the members also sought political office, as evidence by the election of A.T. Walden to the Democratic Committee in the 1950s. In 1963, attorney Leroy Johnson became the first African American elected to the Georgia House of Representative since Reconstruction. He, along with three other lawyers—Donald Hollowell, Wiley Branton, and A.T. Walden—attended a meeting of the National Bar with President John F. Kennedy to discuss the nation's civil rights problem.

By 1965, there were 5,000 white lawyers in Georgia and 34 African-American lawyers. Concerned about the small number of African-American lawyers in the city, attorney Wesley M. Mathews, who had began his practice in Atlanta in 1953, organized the Mathews School of Law three years earlier to aid in training men and women who desired to pursue a career in law. The school was located at 197 1/2 Auburn Avenue.

The decade of the 1970s was a flurry of activity. Members of the GCBA and some 50 African-American applicants called on Gov. Jimmy Carter and the U.S. Justice Department to investigate alleged discrimination in the failure of all black applicants out of 254 who took the in the Georgia Bar exam in 1972. Marvin Arrington, then an aid, led the protest requesting that the five-man state board be replaced. State Senator Leroy Johnson vowed to introduce legislation to the Georgia Assembly that would provide a ten-man board with a split black and white membership.

By the 1980s, issues for the GCBA included placing an African American to the Georgia Board of Bar Examiners, a five-member group responsible for preparing the state bar examination as well as grading it. Attorney Charles S. Johnson, a former secretary and president, was sworn in on October 25, 1982, fulfilling one of Gate City's goals. The publication of the organization's own magazine, *The Nexus,* proved to be a significant milestone for the organization as a forum was created to intellectually discuss those legal strides and gains that affected African-American lawyers.

Even in the 1990s, discrimination still ranked as a major issue. In 1992, black members of the State Bar of Georgia threatened to create a Georgia Alliance of African-American Attorneys. The bylaws of the state bar were changed in 1991 to allow the president of the GCBA to serve as an ex-officio member of the board.

For African-American female lawyers, the 1990s produced long overdue gains. Thelma Wyatt Cummings Moore (pictured with Mayor Maynard Jackson) was appointed the first African-American woman in Georgia to serve on the State

Court Bench. Judge Moore also was the first woman to serve full time on the benches of the Atlanta Municipal Court, the city court. In February of 1992, Leah Sears Collins was appointed by Governor Zell Miller as the first African-American woman to the Georgia Supreme Court.

Now some 50 years later, the GCBA has fulfilled its mission of creating, in the Atlanta community, an appreciation for the legal profession. Its past leadership has been stellar and includes A.T. Walden, T.J. Henry, R.E. Thomas, S.B. Wright, R. Prudence Herndon, Edward S. D'Antignac, Donald Hollowell, Julius C. Daughtery, Romae T. Powell, Horace T. Ward, John L. Kennedy, Felker S. Ward, Thomas G. Sampson, Charles S. Johnson III, James Booker, Antonio Thomas, Lenwood A. Jackson, Linwood R. Slayton, Jr., W. Roy Mays III, Donald P. Edwards, Kevin A. Ross, P. Andrew Patterson, Janice L. Miller, R. David Ware, Willie E. Robinson, Josie Alexander, Alvarita Hanson, James Finley, Ronald Freeman, Ronald Mangham, Patrise Perkins Hooker, and H. Michael Harvey.

Former and current Gate City members are represented highly in all aspects of the law, government, and the political arena. There are hundreds of black-owned law firms throughout the metropolitan Atlanta area. Members of this organization helped to create the Georgia Association of Black Women Attorneys, often referred to as GABWA. Though the promised land has not been crossed completely, as founder A.T.Walden once remarked, members of the GCBA believe that they have reached a pinnacle in history where there is surely "light at the end of the tunnel."

SOME SIGNIFICANT EVENTS IN THE HISTORY OF AFRICAN-AMERICAN LAWYERS IN ATLANTA, 1870–1975

"Must Morehouse students, must all the colored youth of Atlanta, of Georgia, forever go about in terror of their lives?"

—John Hope, *c.* 1930

• 1872: Charlotte E. Ray becomes the first woman law graduate from Howard University.

• 1930: The Black Shirts hold their first mass rally and, five days later, lynch Dennis Hubert, driver of John Hope and son of Rev. G. Johnson Hubert. Hubert was falsely accused of raping a white girl. Africans Americans in Atlanta organize to protest the murder and are met with repercussions when Rev. Hubert's home is burned to the ground. Churches collecting funds for the prosecution are teargassed. Following a grand jury investigation, attorney Austin T. Walden helps convict the accused killers of Dennis Hubert.

• January 1956: Mrs. Ruth M. Ramsey, a secretary at the university and the John Hope Homes housing project, is selected as the first African-American woman to serve on the Fulton County grand jury.

• 1965: The first graduating class of Mathews School of Law holds its commencement exercises at the Allen Temple AME Church. The graduates are Irvin G. Britt, Mildred Felder, Emma P. Gooden, Katheryn R. Williams, Wallace J. Gooden, Jonathan W. Horne, and Louise B. Hornsby.

• 1964: Attorney William Alexander files a federal suit against future governor Lester Maddox charging that his act violates the 1964 Civil Rights Act.

• 1967: Marvin Arrington and Clarence Cooper graduate from the Emory Law School.

•1968: Attorney Clarence Cooper, a graduate of Emory University Law School, is appointed as the first African-American assistant district attorney in Fulton County.

•May 1969: Attorneys Maynard H. Jackson (a candidate for vice mayor) and William Alexander (a state representative) attempt to become members of the exclusive Atlanta Lawyers Club. They are met with ten blackballs each and are dropped from consideration.

•January 1973: Mrs. Romae Turner Powell is selected by the superior court judges of Fulton County to serve as a county juvenile court judge replacing Judge John Langford.

•January 1973: Fifteen black law school graduates file a federal suit seeking to prohibit the Georgia State Board of Examiners and four superior court clerks form enforcing Georgia laws requiring passage of state law board exams to be licensed to practice in the state. The plaintiffs of the suit are James E.C. Perry, Jack LaSonde, Marvin Nathaniel Clark, Ben T. Cole, Jacqueline Bennett, Melvin Robinson, Ronald Stewart, Marvin Mangham, Cecil Pace, Thomas F. Bingley, Thulani Walter Gabashe, Joseph Arrington, Rutha L. Bradley, Orin L. Alexis, and Bruce L. Perkins. Representing the plaintiffs are Marvin Arrington, C.B. King of Albany, Bobby Hill of Savannah, Thomas Jackson of Macon, and Emily Carson of Atlanta.

•1973: John M. Turner, Jr., a graduate of the National Law Center of George Washington University and Morris Brown College, is appointed as the assistant U.S. attorney in the division of contraband and organized crime.

•January 30, 1975: Mayor Maynard Jackson appoints 31-year-old attorney Mary Welcome the city's first municipal court solicitor. She is a graduate of the Howard University Law School.

In May of 1953, George Prather (above) was beaten by three white deputies at the State Farmers Market on Lee Street and Murphy Avenue. The incident occurred after some words were passed between Prather and the deputies while they were stuck in a traffic jam. The deputies followed him and his mother down a street and declared they intended to teach him "how to talk to white men," then proceeded to beat him up. After the attack, Prather was placed under arrest of charges of disorderly conduct, resisting arrest, and swearing and was placed in Hughes Spaulding Pavillion for treatment of a broken nose and head, hand, facial, and body injuries. The charges were dismissed after his counsel, attorney Dan Duke, pointed out that they had no jurisdiction to make an arrest outside of the market. After suing in civil court, he was awarded $1,000 in damages before the trial began. He had initially asked for $10,000.

Pictured is NAACP attorney Constance Baker Motley with attorney Donald L. Hollowell. Hollowell moved to Atlanta in 1942 while serving in the armed services as a commissioned officer and began practicing in 1952 when he and Cassandra E. Maxwell opened their law offices at 864 Hunter Street. A graduate of Loyola University and Lane College, Hollowell became one of the most compassionate civil rights attorneys in Atlanta. In 1964, he made a run for judge of the superior court. His life story was penned in his biography, written by his wife, Mrs. Louise Hollowell, a former professor of English at Morris Brown College.

NAACP attorney Thurgood Marshall was a frequent visitor to Atlanta. In November of 1955, Marshall told an overflow crowd at Wheat Street Baptist Church, who contributed $1,300 towards the NAACP Legal defense fund, that "Desegregation is like washing dirty dishes. I have been house broken long enough to know that you've got to wash dishes. You can put off washing dishes until next morning or next week but the only thing you'll get unless you wash the dishes are cock roaches." He said the trend and new strategy of pro-segregationists was to try and divide and defeat moves towards desegregation by appealing to church people to ignore the NAACP and keep peace and harmony and segregation by working through the preachers and their congregations.

Vernon Eulion Jordan Jr. (shown with Vice President Hubert Humphrey) grew up in Atlanta, having been born on August 15, 1935, to Vernon E. Jordan, a postal clerk at Ft. McPherson, and Mary Griggs Jordan, a caterer. His childhood was spent in University Homes. As a teenager, he worked with his mother in the catering business and even worked at the Lawyers Club of Atlanta. Jordan graduated from David T. Howard High School in 1953, and upon graduation from Depauw University, he enrolled in Howard University Law School. He completed his law degree in 1960 and was admitted to the Georgia Bar. After law school, Jordan returned back to his home in Atlanta and worked for the Hollowell law firm, then on Hunter Street, as a law clerk and did much of the research that enabled the litigation to force the University of Georgia to desegregate. In 1961, he became the Georgia field secretary for the NAACP and, for two years, coordinated efforts among its branches.

Seven

THE FABULOUS FIFTIES?

Jim Crow was alive and well in Atlanta in public transportation, eating facilities, and the school system during the 1950s. Shown above is one of the Jim Crow buses of the Atlanta Transit System in 1956, following the Supreme Court's decision that outlawed segregation on all public buses. State officials said that Georgia was not a party to the South Carolina legal action and would not be immediately affected. Then city attorney Jack Savage said Atlanta had no ordinance actually requiring segregation but did have an ordinance requiring those in charge of buses and trolley to obey the state segregation laws.

71

Left: Dr. Rufus E. Clement, president of Atlanta University, was elected the first African American to serve on the Atlanta Board of Education.

Below: In 1952, the Supreme Court was approached by four states, Kansas, South Carolina, Virginia, and Delaware, and the District of Columbia, who challenged that the segregation in public schools was unconstitutional. African-American students in Atlanta attended segregated schools such as the Booker T. Washington (pictured), David T. Howard, and Henry McNeal Turner High Schools during the 1950s. After the Supreme Court unanimously declared that "separate educational facilities are inherently unequal" and mandated the school districts to operate under one district for all students, the *Brown* decision gave a concentrated voice to the federal government in matters of education policy. Prior to this ruling, matters of policy were left to states and school districts, to the disadvantage of African-American students. The *Brown* decision also set the stage for more aggressive centralized decision-making at the federal level, and for Congress to pass the Civil Rights Acts of 1964 and the Elementary and Secondary Education Act of 1965. Basically, the *Brown* decision was a stepping stone for equality in America.

Dr. Hamilton Holmes, his sons Oliver and Alfred "Tup" (standing, left), and businessman C.T. Bell filed a lawsuit in response to the discrimination toward blacks playing on the public golf courses in Atlanta. The Supreme Court upheld, in November 1955, a ruling that declared racial segregation in city or state-owned parks and beaches unconstitutional. It also ruled that the plaintiffs must be admitted to the courses, overturning an earlier decision. As a result, the city of Atlanta was ordered to open its public golf courses to blacks. Mayor Hartsfield stated that the city would comply with the court rule. "If the decision was to close the courses nearly 70,000 white players and 100 city employees would be deprived of their rights and jobs in order to deny a few Negro players the use of the golf links. Swimming pools and playgrounds were not affected." The only opposition came from Alderman Milton G. Farris, who suggested that city lease its golf course to avoid compliance to the ruling. He also suggested asking black leaders to agree to a compromise and set aside certain days for "Negro" golfers. Gov. Marvin Griffin suggested the same on a state level. Virgil Hodges, chairman of the Atlanta NAACP Executive Committee, responded "We turned down the compromise a long time ago."

Attorney Austin T. Walden and Miles Amos are shown here. Both were elected to the City Executive Committee in 1953.

Outspoken and charismatic congressman Adam Clayton Powell spoke at the 1956 commencement of Morehouse College. He is followed by Dr. Benjamin Elijah Mays, president of Morehouse College. Among the students graduating in that class were Maynard Holbrook Jackson, who would become Atlanta's first African-American mayor, and A. Reginald Eaves, Atlanta's first African-American police chief.

The Dixie Hill Express bus company was privately owned by African Americans. It picked up and transported its riders to places the Atlanta Transit Company did not serve.

Pictured here is a campaign poster for Mrs. Ruby Blackburn. Mrs. Blackburn, along with Miss Hattie Holmes, qualified to run for the Fulton County Democratic Executive Committee in the September 10, 1958 primary.

In what was known as the "Triple L Movement" in January of 1957, six African-American ministers boarded a bus with the intention of sitting in the usually reserved white seats. The ministers—William Holmes Borders, Robert H. Shorts (CME), A. Franklin Fisher, Howard Bussy, B.J. Johnson (Mt. Calvary Baptist), and R.H. Williams—were arrested and hauled away in a paddy wagon for violating Georgia segregation laws in occupying public bus seats up front, which were normally reserved for white passengers. They were jailed temporarily until they posted $1,000 bond each. Following their release, Borders (shown below exiting a police wagon) spoke to a crowd of about 1,200 and informed them that the campaign

against segregated bus seating would "go forward at whatever the cost." The next day, the driver of the bus pulled to the curb claiming he had "mechanical trouble." So intense was the event, that Governor Griffin alerted the Georgia militia to be on standby.

Rev. Samuel Williams, pastor of the Friendship Baptist Church, and John Porter filed a law suit against the transportation company. U.S. District Court judge Frank A. Hooper ruled that that Atlanta's segregated seating on public transportation was outlawed, but the plaintiffs were not given an injunctive relief.

As a result of these efforts, Atlanta's public bus transportation was integrated on January 22, 1959. A public rally was held in which African-American men were told they could sit where they pleased but to use judgement in sitting next to white women.

Eight
BLACK POWER
COMES TO ATLANTA

"What do you want? Black Power!"
—Stokley Carmichael, c. 1966

"Atlanta can count on intensified demonstrations in the near future."
—James Forman (following the Summerhill Race Riot of 1966)

On September 11, 1960, the Honorable Elijah Muhammad appeared at the Magnolia Ballroom. He is shown with Louis Farrakahn (adjusting the microphone) and Malcom X. It was his only known appearance in Atlanta. Muhammad spoke before some 3,000 African Americans who were inside and outside of the Vine City ballroom. His arrival created a stir, with threats by the Ku Klux Klan. Futile attempts to prevent the meeting including the refusal to the Muslims to use the City Auditorium, which was a larger venue. In addition, Atlanta University officials refused the use of their auditorium, along with several large churches. Finally, the Magnolia Ballroom was rented by its owner, B.B. Beamon, a renowned entertainment promoter, who was questioned by the police after he accepted the offer. City officials found violations on the building and restricted the capacity to 800, according to Wali Muhammad in his book *Muslims in Georgia: A Chronology and Oral History*. Even the police chief called Beamon and told him that he would receive a citation. The chief asked to bug the ballroom so that they could listen, and Beamon agreed. However, the chief did not get their ears worth, for Muhammad did not speak about overthrowing the government. The *Atlanta Constitution* reported that only 1,200 people were in attendance at the Magnolia, and most came from outside of Atlanta. Rallies were often held at the Magnolia Ballroom, including the Black Unity Forum held in March of 1964. Over 650 people attended the forum, where the topic was "Black Unity: The Key to Freedom." The program included a panel of speakers ranging from Rev. Wyatt T. Walker, executive secretary of the SCLC, who left when he learned that the meeting was not opened to whites; attorney Howard Moore Jr.; *Atlanta Inquirer* managing editor Charles A. Black; and Jeremiah Shabazz. Heavyweight boxing champion Muhammad Ali was expected to attend but wired a message from New York to the Atlanta crowd expressing his regrets.

What was the fascination about the Muslims and the Nation of Islam? It was during the times of the Great Depression, which began in 1929 during the administration of President Herbert Hoover. A man (the wise master) came to America from the East. He is believed to have been of Arab descent, but that has not been documented. His first appearance in America was in the ghetto of Detroit. He gave the name of Wallace D. Fard. He first made a living here by selling old clothes from door to door. He would tell stories about the people who wore these clothes, and this would lead to gatherings at homes. It was here that Americans first started hearing his word on their land of origin.

Heavyweight boxing champion Muhammad Ali was a frequent visitor to Atlanta. Here he visits a local mosque, *c.* 1960s.

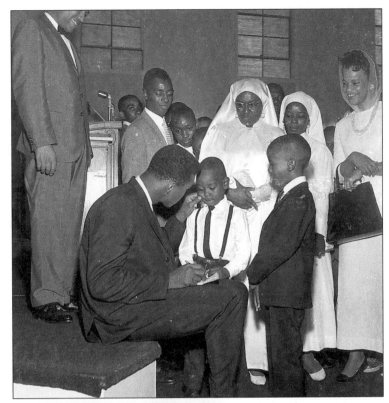

Activist H. Rap Brow and Muhammad Ali converse outside of Paschal's Hotel on Hunter Street, *c.* 1960s.

In the 1960s, Malcom X often visited the Atlanta University Center and spoke to the students. He visited Atlanta on several occasions, including when he accompanied the Honorable Elijah Muhammad and in 1961 when he addressed a math seminar on the Atlanta University campus and spoke about black superiority, criticizing the white race and Christianity. On another occasion, he spoke about the mathematics behind the pyramids and the Sphinx. According to an account, the professors and graduate students were "enraptured . . . on the edge of their sears, drinking every word."

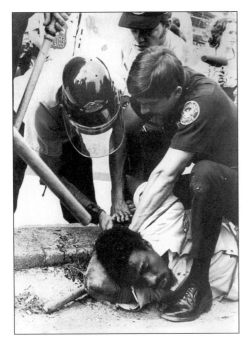

On Tuesday, September 6, 1966, around 1:18 p.m., the day after Labor Day, a violent riot broke out in Atlanta's oldest African-American neighborhood, Summerhill. The riot was triggered by the shooting of 25-year-old auto larceny suspect Harold Louis Prather as he tried to avoid arrest by a uniformed Atlanta police officer. African-American policemen in Atlanta were dispatched to the scene but were unable to control the excited crowd. A few hours later, Stokely Carmichael and some fellow SNCC workers joined the riot. Over a period of time, the crowd became more violent and agitated when white policemen moved in, and residents began to throw bottles, stones, and bricks. Policemen retaliated by using guns, tear gas, and billy clubs. By nightfall, police had quadrooned the area and dispersed the crowd with tear gas and by shooting their pistols in the air. Several people were injured, and over 30 arrests were made.

As Mayor Ivan Allen walked the streets of the Summerhill neighborhood to help insure peace, rioters began to rock the car where the victim had been holstered. Shouts of profanity and the echoes of "black power" were heard. African-American men in the community urged Allen to release those who had been jailed, and demanded that the white officers be removed from the area. Following the outbreaks, a group of citizens met with three members of the Atlanta Aldermanic Board, including Richard Freeman, chairman of the board, Vice Mayor Sam Massell, and Q.V. Williamson, to formulate plans to ease tension in the Summerhill area. The committee agreed that the Student Non Violent Coordinating Committee (SNCC) was not wanted in the area for any assistance. In addition, discourteous white and "negro" policemen

would be removed from the Capital Avenue area; a white and "negro" officer would patrol the section on foot together as long as they were courteous; the city sanitary department would clean up the area with street sweepers; and a recreation area for teens and young adults would be developed.

After attending Howard University in the early 1960s, Stokely Carmichael found himself on the battleground of the South, attempting to integrate buses and terminals as a freedom rider. As a member of the SNCC, he and his cadre registered close to 4,000 voters in Alabama. He was arrested at midnight on Thursday, September 8, 1966, on charges of inciting the riot that broke out in Summerhill. Just before his arrest, he was elected chairman of the SNCC. James Forman came from Philadelphia to take command of the group in his absence and issued a bitter statement against Mayor Allen, the police department, and the U.S. war efforts in Vietnam in a press conference at the SNCC headquarters. He was later released and freed on $1,000 bond during the proceedings. Four nights later, a 14-year-old black male, Herbert Vorner, was murdered in a similar disturbance. Shortly afterwards, Carmichael left the county for a five-month tour that included stops in Cuba and Hanoi. If he was convicted of this misdemeanor, it carried a penalty of a year in jail. Gov. Lester Maddox planned to ask the legislature to increase the penalty by raising the crime to felony. In addition to these charges, Carmichael was also to be prosecuted for draft law violations; he was a vocal opponent of the draft.

81

Local residents watch a Ku Klux Klan demonstration going through Summerhill, c. 1960s. The Klan's history went back to December of 1865, in Pulaski, near the Alabama border of Tennessee. Six young men, who had been officers in the Civil War, decided to form a club. Initially, they were indecisive about what name they should choose—"the Jolly Six" and "the Thespians" are examples of names that they considered. They eventually decided to use the Greek word for circle, *kuklos*. The group met in secret places, put on disguises, and had great fun galloping around town after dark. They soon discovered that their nightly appearances had an unexpected affect of fear, on which they capitalized. The Klan portrayed themselves as ghastly, ghostly figures who had not drank water since the battles of the Civil War. These images and folk tales served as a catalyst of fear amongst the newly freed slaves of the south. The Klan's motive soon changed from fraudulent horse play to controlling free Negroes. At first, there was no thought of violence, but this soon changed. The Klan was attracting widespread attention, and soon branched off from the small town of Pulaski.

In April 1867, representatives met in Nashville, TN, at the Maxwell House. During this meeting, a constitution, or a prescript, was drawn up. In this manuscript, the Klan inscribed clauses to protect the weak and innocent of the South. Gen. Nathan Bedford Forrest of the Confederate Army was elected Grand Wizard.

The Klan soon became a combination of discipline and irresponsibility. They boasted that they were a "rough bunch of boys"—they threatened, shot, stabbed, hung, and destroyed. They drove Northerners from the South, and attacked officials who registered blacks and those who did not give whites priority over blacks. Active in nine states from Tennessee to the Carolinas, to Mississippi, Arkansas, and Texas, the Klan generally operated in the upland areas, in the part of the South where blacks formed a lesser percentage of the population. Although the Klan was initially composed of and led by wealthier citizens, it eventually represented a cross section of the population.

By 1869, the Klan was experiencing internal trouble. The organization proved to be impossible to control. The wealthier citizens were dropping out, and the quality of membership was declining. Forrest ordered publicly that the Klan be dissolved, and all of its records be burned. The Klan was brought to a halt.

CORE (Congress of Racial Equality) was an interracial organization dedicated to promoting civil rights in the United States. This organization was formed in Chicago in 1942 by James Farmer. The goal of CORE was to envision a national movement based on nonviolence, and it was directed toward the area of segregated public accommodations. CORE began staging sit-ins at restaurants in the 1940s.

During the 1950s, CORE expanded its efforts to combat discrimination in employment. Experimenting with direct action techniques, such as picketing and boycotting target stores, CORE attempted to open up new job opportunities for African Americans in retail stores in African-American neighborhoods. In 1958, the organization conducted the first successful black boycott campaign, directed against a St. Louis bread manufacturer.

In 1961, CORE gained national attention with its sponsorship of the Freedom Ride into the Deep South. Biracial members of CORE participated in a bus ride through Alabama and Mississippi, with the purpose of challenging segregation in interstate bus travel. The Freedom Ride represented a continuation of the policy of direct action and confrontation. Members of CORE were received with hostility and encountered violence and jail sentences.

After the first freedom rides, CORE was involved with other civil rights projects, such as voter registration drives and "Freedom Schools" in the South, and established projects in urban ghettos in the North. In 1966, Floyd B. McKissick succeeded as national director of CORE, and the organization became more militant in its approach to racial problems. McKissick endorsed the concept of "black power," which became widespread in the African-American community. "Black power" meant resorting to violence under certain conditions. It was an assertion by African Americans toward greater control over their own affairs and over the Civil Rights Movement. The adoption of the "black power" slogan by CORE changed this organization's long-standing commitment to nonviolence in favor of a new policy of self-defense.

While adopting "black power," CORE believed that "leadership, planning, and the implementation of policy should logically be in the hands of blacks." In politics, CORE felt that African Americans should rule whenever they constituted a majority. They also believed that in the traditional American two-party system, African Americans could possibly constitute an important third force, "especially in the black ghettos of large cities," places where increasing concentrations of African Americans threatened the old political arrangements.

By 1967, the Black Panther Party and the Black Power movement had spread to the South and to Atlanta. Rallies were held throughout the city, and young student activists from the Atlanta University Center School were actively involved.

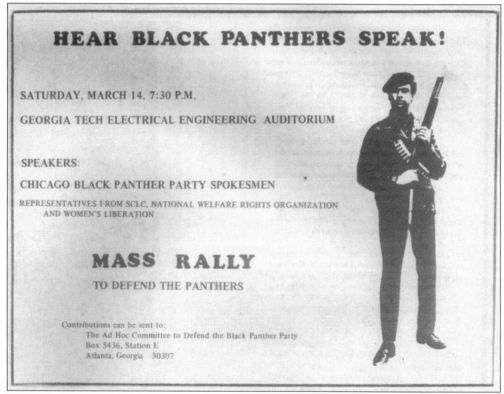

This poster promotes a Black Panther rally at the Georgia Tech Auditorium on March 14, 1970.

Angela Davis enters an unidentified site to attend a press conference, *c.* 1971.

Seated, from left to right, C.B. King, Angela Davis, Rev. Ralph David Abernathy, and attorney Howard Moore join other civil rights activists including Hosea Williams at a press conference in Atlanta to announce Moore's representation of Angela Davis at her trial in California in 1971.

Chief of Police John Inman was the subject of an verbal attack by the African-American community because of the racist and brutal actions of the Atlanta Police Department toward African Americans in Atlanta.

On Tuesday, November 3, 1970, over 500 marchers gathered at the M.L. King memorial site, next to Ebenezer Baptist Church, and then filed into the streets of Auburn Avenue led by Hosea Williams and Tyrone Brooks. The marchers protested down Auburn Avenue for the removal of Inman, following the killing of 15-year-old Andre Moore, who was gunned down by policemen on the streets of his community. In the weeks and months to follow, two policemen were exonerated by an all-white jury in Fulton County Superior Court and acquitted of charges against them in the slaying. The marchers stopped at the Atlanta police headquarters, then marched through the busy downtown area during lunch, then to the Fulton County Courthouse and Atlanta City Hall.

No publication of Atlanta's Civil Rights Movement would be complete without the inclusion its legendary son, Martin Luther King, Jr. Some of King's early influence came from the weekly lectures presented in the Sale Hall Chapel during his student days at Morehouse College. Dr. King is shown above, at the far left, listening to one of the numerous speakers President Mays would bring to the campus, or to one of Dr. Mays's own lectures, *c.* 1947.

Dr. King is shown here at the old Atlanta Airport with Rev. Ralph David Abernathy (center) and his brother, Alfred Daniel King, *c.* 1960s.

Dr. Martin Luther King, Jr., greets Gov. Nelson Rockerfeller in Atlanta as Mayor Ivan Allen (center) looks on. Also shown are Dr. Benjamin Mays (far left), daughter Yolanda, Mrs. Coretta Scott King, and Mrs. Rachel Robinson. Jackie Robinson is hidden by Governor Rockerfeller, *c.* 1965.

King confers with *Atlanta Daily World* editor C.A. Scott at an unidentified event, *c.* 1960s.

In the early 1960s, Rev. Ralph David Abernathy accepted the invitation to pastor the West Hunter Street Baptist Church, and the Abernathy family moved to Atlanta.

Ralph David Abernathy was born on March 11, 1926, to Louivery and W.L. Abernathy. He was the youngest of 10 children. When he was 12, he got the name Ralph David Abernathy from older sister Manerva, after one of her favorite professors. As is stated in his autobiography, Ralph David Abernathy was Joshua to Martin Luther King, Jr.'s Moses. He was at Martin Luther King, Jr.'s side during all the battles, and he eventually became his successor.

When Rosa Parks was arrested in 1956 for not giving up her seat on a Montgomery Alabama bus, Abernathy enlisted Martin Luther King, Jr., to join the protest. Together, they headed the landmark bus

boycott for 381 days. During this time, Abernathy's house was bombed, and his church was dynamited. He, however, continued to push. Both Abernathy and King helped found the Southern Christian Leadership Conference (SCLC). Abernathy was jailed more than 40 times along with King in their nonviolent quest. His mission took him all over the South; he visited Selma, Albany, and Birmingham, as well as Washington and Chicago. In 1968, when Martin Luther King, Jr., was assassinated, he died in Abernathy's arms. During that sorrowful period, Abernathy took up the reins of the nonviolent movement. The following January, Abernathy led the Poor People's March on Washington, D.C., which had been planned by King. Abernathy was succeeded by Rev. Joseph Lowery, who led the SCLC into the decades of the 80s and 90s.

The banquet honoring Rev. Dr. Martin Luther King, Jr., for receiving the Nobel Peace Prize was held at the Biltmore Hotel in 1965. Dr. King is shown talking to his father, Rev. M.L. "Daddy" King, Sr.

The SCLC embodied the vision and philosophy of its founding president, Dr. Martin Luther King, Jr. (shown at left leaving the Atlanta headquarters in the Prince Hall Masonic Building on the corner of Auburn Avenue and Hilliard Street), as well as the hopes and aspirations of countless community leaders and local activists. Individuals representing varied political, social, religious, and ideological backgrounds came together to challenge racism. King's philosophy of nonviolent direct action and his vision for a mass movement based on Christian tenets of love and understanding guided the activities of the SCLC. A seemingly endless cascade of demonstrations, marches, boycotts, and sit-ins confronted the practice of Southern racism. Occasionally, the demonstrators were beaten back. Occasionally, they were met with only token concessions. Cumulatively, however, their campaigns wore down the defense of Jim Crow and energized the African-American community in the South to address the issues of place and access. Although there were precursors to this vision, nonviolent direct action became a major force in American politics for the first time under the leadership of King and the SCLC.

During the movement in Atlanta, many national entertainers offered to put on concerts to raise money for the movement in what was billed "Stars for Freedom." Mahalia Jackson was a favorite of Dr. King and performed often in Atlanta, including a concert in December of 1963 at the City Auditorium.

To raise funds for the SCLC, noted entertainers like Lena Horne, Ray Charles, Tony Bennett, Ella Fitzgerald, and others performed under the bill "Stars for Freedom."

* Dick Gregory
* Johnny Mathis
* Lena Horne
* Ray Charles
* Marlon Brando
* Tony Bennett
* Danny Kaye
* Sammy Davis
* Ella Fitzgerald
* Eddie Fisher
* Harry Belafonte

STARS FOR FREEDOM

1963-64

Southern Christian Leadership Conference 50

Sammy Davis, Jr., gave a benefit performance at the City Auditorium in 1966. He and Dr. King were very good friends.

Following a benefit concert by Harry Belafonte, guests were invited to a private reception at the home of businessman T.M. Alexander on Hunter Street. Seated in Alexander's living room are Rev. King, Harry Belafonte, and T.M. Alexander, Sr. Standing are an unidentified man and T.M. Alexander, Jr. Dr. King is pictured listening to Mrs. Harry Belafonte during the reception.

The outpour of unity that the assassination and funeral of Martin Luther King, Jr., in April of 1968 brought the citizens of Atlanta is unlike anything the city had ever seen. The double mule-drawn wagon carrying the remains of King, moved from Ebenezer through the streets of Atlanta, ending up at Morehouse College, where another service was held.

Nine
INTEGRATING SCHOOLS

On Friday, June 5, 1959, two federal judges, Hooper and Sloan, issued a decision that declared segregation in the Atlanta public school system unconstitutional. The ruling came as a result of a suit filed by 10 parents of children enrolled in the system, following several years of court activity. Mrs. Constance Baker Motley (an NAACP lawyer) presented the case along with attorneys E.E. Moore and A.T. Walden. Motley began arguments attempting to convince the court that an immediate plan of desegregation of schools should be ordered by the court. The Atlanta Public School system was to be integrated or else closed by September of 1959. Nine students, accompanied by African-American policemen in civilian dress, integrated Atlanta high schools including Murphy, Northside, Brown, and Grady. There were no major disturbances, though four white students were arrested for disturbing the peace. By 1967, all grades were integrated.

Henry McNeal Turner High School students Charlyne Hunter and Hamilton Holmes (shown at their graduation from UGA in 1963) were approached to integrate Georgia State University, but later decided that they would try to integrate the University of Georgia. On January 11, 1961, a riot broke out following the suspension of Holmes and Hunter to the University of Georgia. They were later reinstated under a court order on January 16. Their accomplishment was landmark. During Reconstruction, several freedmen tried to attend the university, and in 1939, three African Americans applied. The most celebrated case included the attempt by Horace Ward, who tried to enter the university law school. After their first quarter, Holmes made the honor roll. Mary Frances Early, who worked one time as a camp director at Allatoona, became the first African American accepted to attend graduate school at the University of Georgia.

The first African-American graduates of Emory University master's program were Verdelle Bellamy and Allie Saxon, both of whom completed the master's program in nursing, *c.* 1964.

Kerry Rushin (center) became the first African-American student to enter the University of Georgia as a freshman. She is shown receiving a scholarship check from Mrs. Alice Washington (left) and Mrs. J.R. Wilson of the Atlanta chapter of Jack and Jill, *c.* 1964.

THE
⬛ATLANTA INQUIRER

"To seek out the Truth and report it without Fear or Favor"

| VOL. ONE | TEL. 5-3-6087 | ATLANTA, GEORGIA, SATURDAY, MAY 13, 1961 | TEN CENTS | No. 42 |

GEORGIA TECH ACCEPTS 3 NEGROES

☆ ☆ ☆ ☆ ☆

U. Of Ga. Grad School Accepts Local Teacher

MISS MAROON AND WHITE 1961-'62. Brenda Sue Hill, a Spelman sophomore, was elected Miss Maroon and White by the Morehouse student body recently. Miss Hill, an English major and a French minor, is a native of Gladewater, Texas, a member of the Spelman Glee Club and Orchestra, and was also elected president of the Spelman Student

10 REJECTED

The Inquirer learned early Thursday afternoon that three Negroes have been mailed tentative acceptances to the Georgia Institute of Technology. If accepted, they will be the first of their race to attend the 76-year-old formerly all-white school.

(See story on applicants, page 12.)

Official sources list the names of three as Ralph A. Long, Lawrence Williams, and Ford Greene. Two are from Turner High School and one is from Washington High.

President Edwin D. Harrison, in a prepared statement, said, "So far this year, the Georgia Institute of Technology has mailed 1,000 tentative acceptances to prospective freshmen for the fall quarter 1961. We normally designate these acceptances "tentative" contingent on satisfactory completion of high school or preparatory school programs.

Among those students mailed tentative acceptances, were three members of the Negro race. Among those rejected were ten

(Continued on Page 2)

Miss Early Camping With Youngsters As Acceptance Is Announced

When the long awaited official news came that Mary Frances Early had been admitted as the first of her race to attend graduate school at the University of Georgia, the talented and able young teacher was not at home to receive the news. Typically, she was serving as camp director at Allatoona. Entrusted to her care as director, along with eight other counsellors, were 101 students, grades 5-7, from various schools in the Atlanta area.

Her mother, Mrs. John Henry Early, informed by telephone of the word that had come from the head of the Board of Regents, said, "I'm happy for her sake that it's
(Continued on Page 16)

The headline for the *Atlanta Inquirer* on May 13, 1961, announces the acceptance of three African Americans into the Georgia Institute of Technology (Georgia Tech). The students were Ralph A. Long Jr., Lawrence Williams, and Ford Greene.

In 1967, Marvin Arrington became one of the first African-American graduates of Emory University Law School. Arrington, a graduate of Turner High School, was elected to the Atlanta City Council in the 1970s.

Seated are the principal players in the University of Georgia integration suit: Hamilton Holmes, attorney Horace Ward, attorney Austin T. Walden, Rev. W.W. Witherspoon, and Milton White(standing), president of the Eta Lambda Alpha Phi Alpha Fraternity, Inc.

Jesse Hill, along with Grace T. Hamilton and Clarence Coleman of the Atlanta Urban League and Rev. Samuel Williams, became the star witnesses in the Georgia state case that was finally won. Hill also directed the recruiting efforts for students to desegregate Georgia colleges and universities.

Teacher integration in Atlanta public schools began in 1965, when West Fulton High School received its first African-American counselor. In the fall of 1968, Deloris Harris Conley and Helen Stovall, two teachers at the all-black Thomas Heathe Slater School, accepted voluntary transfer and integrated the all-white Lester R. Brewer Elementary School. They were two of hundreds of African-American teachers in Atlanta that helped to integrate the Atlanta Public School System.

Ten

STUDENT PROTEST: THE SNCC AND COAHR

During the 1960s, civil rights were being challenged not just by African-American adults, but also by the students who studied at the various black colleges and universities. It made perfect sense; this was the world they were about to enter into as professionals. For them, they saw limited opportunities to grow as individuals and into a race. They had to make a change. Stimulated by the student lunch counter sit-in in Alabama on February 1, 1960, the Atlanta University Center decided it was now time for them to join the ranks of protest. Comprised of Morris Brown, Clark, Morehouse, and Spelman Colleges, the Atlanta University Center gave endless efforts to make the city of Atlanta realize a change was about to occur. The students of the AUC came together, made strategies on boycotts and lunch counter sit-ins, and organized the Committee on Appeal for Human Rights (COAHR).

On March 15, 1960, the first widespread sit-in occurred. This resulted in the arrest of 77 Atlanta University related students. They were arrested under the new Georgia trespassing law. While protesting, the students faced opposition at first with college presidents and teachers who warned them of the dangers of rebellion. Despite their teachers' notions, the students carried on. In celebration of the U.S. Supreme Court's 1954 anti-segregation, the students gathered and proceeded to march to the State Capitol Building in downtown Atlanta, but were diverted by Atlanta police so that students would not meet head on with the angry mobs that awaited them.

Students in their prime of protest manned picket lines against food stores that had a large number of black clients but refused to hire African Americans above the menial levels such as dish boys. Students also met with the city's leading department store, which was Rich's at the time. During this private meeting with the department store president, he suggested that students give up the fight. The students were angered by the president's statements and firmly said they would boycott him as well. The president then shouted in turn by saying, " I don't need Negro trade!" The city of Atlanta was beginning to feel the burn of the students.

Some of the courageous students in the Atlanta University Center who led the movement included Carolyn Long, Wilma Long, Ben Brown, Brenda Hill Cole, Joi Thompson, Lonnie King, Rudy Doris Smith, Mary Ann Smith, Ruth Barett, Willie Mays, James Felder, Marlon D. Bennett, Don Clarke, Roslyn Pope, Herschelle Sullivan, Charles Black, John Gibson, Morris Dillard, Joe Pierce, Frank Holloway, Robert Mants, Joe Felder, Frank Smith, Danny Mitchell, Marion Wright, Johnny Parham, Leon Greene, Ralph Moore, and Lydia Tucker.

Although the school year was officially over, major student leaders continued to make plans for the next year. This was mainly under the direction of a man from Morehouse named Lonnie King. He was co-chaired by a young lady from Spelman, Herschelle Sullivan. Otis Moss, a student at Morehouse, was field commander of the leading commandant. His wife also participated in the movement in 1960. The reopening of the colleges for the year of 1961 was more racially tense than the year before. Not even with the mayor's intentions of a 30-day peace did violence stop. Violence sprung everywhere. Students felt the beatings of opponents such as Emory University and the Ku Klux Klan. The students of these black colleges of Atlanta pressed on in their belief . No longer were they willing to adjust their aspirations and their behavior to a system that saw them only as second-class citizens. Here, Lonnie C. King kneels at an Atlanta police car to confer with jailed student leaders. He would later leave to study law at Howard University. (Courtesy of the *Atlanta Inquirer*.)

With issues arising, the papers of Atlanta caught the spirit of the youth and the community, including the *Atlanta Journal*, *Atlanta Constitution*, and most importantly, the *Atlanta Inquirer* and the A*tlanta Daily World,* which were black publications. The opinions of the students were made known in Atlanta and all over the nation. Their true voice was captured when they wrote, "We, the students of Clark, Morehouse, Morris Brown, and Spelman colleges, Atlanta University and Interdenominational Theological Center—have joined our hearts, minds, and bodies in the cause of gaining those rights which are inherently ours as members of the human race and as citizens of the United States . . . Today's youth will not sit by submissively while being denied all rights, privileges, and joys of life . . ." Members of the Student Non Violent Coordinating Committee are pictured at their office. On the floor is Ruby Doris Smith. Standing is James Foreman.

Students lead Ruby Doris Smith away from the Atlanta Airport after her return from 30 days in jail in North Carolina, *c.* 1965.

SNNC executive secretary James Forman is jammed into a paddy wagon by some of Atlanta's African-American policemen, who handled racial demonstrations after white policemen were charged with brutality, *c.* 1965. (Courtesy of the *Atlanta Inquirer*.)

Jim Crow signs, such as the one pictured, were common throughout Atlanta. Rev. Samuel Williams is shown here picketing Rich's Department Store.

On March 9, 1960, a group of Morehouse, Spelman, Clark, and Morris Brown College students known as the Committee on Appeal for Human Rights placed a full-page ad in the *Journal Constitution* entitled "An Appeal for Human Rights." Advertisements such as this "Platform for Freedom" were printed in the *Atlanta Inquirer* to inform the public of meetings and activities of the student movement. The article read, "Todays youth will not sit by submissively while being denied all the rights, privileges, and joys of life. We want to state clearly and unequivocally that we cannot tolerate, in a nation professing democracy and among people professing Christianity, the discriminatory conditions under which the Negro lives today in Atlanta, GA . . . We do not intend to wait placidly for those rights which are already legally and morally ours to be metered out to us one at a time."

The struggle for equality for Americans of African descent continues despite the significant advances made during the 1950s and 1960s. The question arises whether the struggle for civil rights has actually benefited the descendants of the many who sacrificed jobs, properties, reputations, and even their lives. The Civil Rights Act defined the true reason for the Constitution of the United States of America. The act put a long lasting impact on American society. Blacks and whites today use the Civil Rights Act to confirm that justice is still being served.

The sign speaks for itself: "Support the Merchants Who Support Segregation." This unidentified protester pickets on Broad Street near the Rich's building, *c.* 1960s. There were numerous counter demonstrations against African-American protesters.

The picketing of Rich's Department Store brought out unmasked members of the Ku Klan Klan. They are shown here on the side of the building in an attempt to intimidate and counter the protesters.

The Rev. Wyatt Tee Walker (at the podium) led rallies with the SCLC to demonstrate strategies for protests and demonstrations. This meeting, held at the Wheat Street Baptist Church, was one of many held at churches in Atlanta.

Rev. William Holmes Borders (at right, with the microphone) leads a demonstration and rally in the rain on March 26, 1961, at the Herndon Stadium of Morris Brown College.

Rev. Otis Moss, following his graduation from Morehouse College, joined the staff of the Southern Christian Leadership Conference. He was an active member and leader of the student movement.

Employees of the Atlanta Life Insurance Company used their lunch breaks to join picket lines at Rich's and other stores and restaurants that did not allow African Americans to patronize, c. 1960s.

After a sit in demonstration at Rich's Department Store, Dr. Martin Luther King, Jr., and others were taken into custody. He is shown leaving the store following his arrest. Other demonstrations were going on simultaneously at this time.

This sign clearly expresses the resentment of the protesters who demonstrated against Rich's Department Store. Rich's was the target of the largest demonstration of civil rights activists in Atlanta.

A white demonstrator is taunted by a white male during a Rich's protest. Many whites joined the Civil Rights Movement in Atlanta.

Jesse Jackson, founder of the Rainbow Coalition, joined Atlanta Dentist in their protest against discrimination at the Hinman Dental Clinic. The demonstration took place at the Atlanta City Auditorium

The Hinman Dental Clinic claimed that African Americans were not invited because they were not members of the American Dental Association.

African-American dentists in Atlanta protest the Hinman Dental Clinic, *c.* 1960s.

Eleven

THE HUNGRY CLUB AND THE NATIONAL URBAN LEAGUE

Since 1945, lunch meetings at the Butler Street YMCA of concerned African Americans, known as the Hungry Club, have provided a forum to discuss political and civil rights issues. Shown speaking into the microphone is Rev. Martin Luther King, Sr. To the left is Mrs. Alberta King. Seated is Jesse B. Blayton. The Hungry Club's motto was "Food for Taste and Food for Thought for those who hunger for information and association."

Mayor Ivan Allen speaks at the Hungry Club, *c*. 1967. Seated are Q.V. Williamson and John Calhoun. (Photo by Harmon Perry.)

Attorney Horace Ward, speaking *c*. 1960s at the Butler Street YMCA, was a native of Lagrange, GA, and a graduate of Morehouse College and Atlanta University. He was one of the many politicians who used the forum to discuss issues relevant to blacks in Atlanta.

Dr. Martin Luther King, Jr. (center), is joined by his wife, Coretta, and members of his fraternity, Alpha Phi Alpha. The assembly took place following Dr. King's speech at the Hungry Club, *c.* 1967.

Herman Talmedge ,Clayton Yates, William Fowlkes, and Dr. Benjamin E. Mays are pictured at the Hungry Club forum, *c.* 1960s.

Following a Hungry Club meeting, Dr. Benjamin Elijah Mays, Mayor Sam Massell, and contractor Herman Russell confer, *c.* 1971.

Still proclaiming that he is "Unbossed and Unbought," Hosea Williams gives the Hungry Club message in 1987. (Photo by Harmon Perry.)

Between 1910 and 1920, an estimated 500,000 blacks left the South. The blacks who fled from the South soon found that they had not escaped segregation and discrimination. They were confined mainly to overcrowded and dilapidated housing, and they were largely restricted to poorly paid, humble jobs. There were many anti-black riots, such as that in East St. Louis, IL, in 1917. But in the Northern cities, the economic and educational opportunities for blacks were clearly greater than they had been in the rural South. In addition, they were helped by various organizations, such as the National Urban League.

The National Urban League, founded in 1910, is a nonprofit social service and civil rights organization with headquarters in New York City. The organization has 113 affiliates in 34 states and Washington, D.C. The mission of the National Urban League is to assist African Americans in achieving social and economic equality. The organization accomplishes its mission through public education regarding policies that affect African Americans; efforts to promote understanding between races; publication of research into the lives of African Americans; programs in job training, education, and career development; and technical assistance to affiliates.

Initially the league was mostly concerned with providing new jobs for blacks in industry and in aiding Southern migrants who had moved into Northern cities. After World War II, the organization became more directly involved in civil rights issues and in the improvement of employment and housing opportunities for American blacks. Its director from 1961 to 1971 was Whitney M. Young, Jr. He was succeeded by Vernon Jordan, who was replaced in 1982 by John E. Jacob. Hugh B. Price became president in 1994. Locally, several Atlantans have worked at the helm of the Atlanta Urban League, including Jesse O. Thomas, Grace Towns Hamilton, Clarence Coleman, and Lyndon Wade.

Whitney Young considered himself more of a strategist than a demonstrator in the struggle for civil rights. He was born on July 13, 1921, in Lincoln Ridge, KY. His father was president of a boarding school for blacks. Young graduated from that school at the age of 14 and studied at Kentucky State College, earning a premedical degree in 1941. He then entered the Army and studied engineering at MIT. Recognizing the unrealized potential of blacks in the Army, he began a career in race relations. He enrolled at the University of Minnesota and received a master's degree in social work in 1947. For the next seven years, he held positions with the St. Paul, MN, and Omaha, NE, chapters of the NUL. He eventually moved to Atlanta, GA, and served as dean of Atlanta University's school of social work.

Young was noted for his superior leadership and ease in working with corporate leaders, politicians, and fellow civil rights workers. He served on seven presidential commissions and worked closely with President Lyndon Johnson. One of his proposals was a "Marshall Plan" for blacks, which attempted to make up for years of deprivation. Young also authored "To Be Equal" and "Beyond Racism." He died on March 12, 1971, in Lagos, Nigeria.

One of the many Whitney M. Young stands on civil rights and what blacks can do is best stated in this excerpt from his speech, *Freedom and Peace: A Blueprint for Tomorrow*, in 1968.

> The core of the civil rights problem is the matter of achieving equal opportunity for Negroes in the labor market. For it stands to reason that all our other civil rights depend on that one for fulfillment. We cannot afford better education for our children, better housing or medical care unless we have jobs.

The National Urban League and Whitney Young were positive examples of the unlimited potential that African Americans possess and can intelligently utilize in order to assist blacks in their constant struggle for equality in America. Young is pictured above with Lyndon Wade, executive director of the Atlanta office, and Clarance Coleman (far left), former director of the Atlanta Urban League.

Twelve

POLITICS IN ATLANTA

*"This revolutionary change will be accepted with human understanding
and good grace, which is an indication of strong attitudes
of the community of Atlanta."*

—Mayor Ivan Allen (on the dedication of the Firestation 16)

THE ATLANTA INQUIRER

ON GUARD For Human Rights 24 Hours A Day

"To seek out the Truth and report it without Fear or Favor"

Attend The Church Of Your Choice . . . Take Someone With You

VOL 3, NO. 15   ATLANTA, GEORGIA, SATURDAY, NOVEMBER 10, 1962   Price 10¢

JOHNSON BECOMES GEORGIA'S 1ST NEGRO SENATOR IN 92 YEARS

VICTORIOUS LEROY JOHNSON AND CHARLES WELTNER GIVE MUTUAL HANDSHAKES OF THANKS TO MRS. LOTTIE WATKINS

Cong. Dawson In Hospital

Congressman William L. Dawson 76, was rushed from his home in Chicago by plane to the U.S. Naval Hospital at Bethesda, Maryland. The latest report from the Washington office of the powerful Democratic leader was that he was responding well to treatment, but that he was "very tired." The exact nature of his illness has not been disclosed.

Wild speculation has ensured as to who would succeed him in Chicago should his condition force him to resign.

Weltner, 16,102 Negro Votes
O'Callaghan Only 6,722

Attorney Leroy R. Johnson's smashing election victory by a greater than two to one margin over T.M. Alexander, Sr., makes him Georgia's first Negro Senator in 92 years. Dr. C.A. Bacote, a leading authority on Georgia Political History indicates that Mr. Johnson is the fourth Negro to be elected to the Georgia Senate. He lists Alpeoria Bradley, George Wallace and Tunish Campbell as the other senators. No Negro has served in the Georgia senate since 1870. William Rodgers a Negro served in the House until 1907.

Charles L. Weltner soundly defeated republican hopeful Jim O'Callaghan by a 10,243 margin. According to unofficial estimates of Dr. C.A. Bacote and Dr. John Reid, it was Mr.

Weltner's overwhelming strength in the Negro Community that stopped the serious GOP bid for power. The unofficial tabulation gave Mr. Weltner

CONTINUED ON PAGE 16

POSTMASTER STRIPPED OF POWERS
by CHARLES A. BLACK

SWEEPING POST OFFICE CHANGES,

By 1960, African Americans in Atlanta were politically charged up and actively working both on a local, regional, and national level. In October of 1960, the Fulton County Citizens Democratic Club opened the Atlanta campaign headquarters for the Kennedy/Johnson ticket at the Waluhaje Hotel and the Consolidated Mortgage Building. Actively involved in the campaign were Warren Cochranem (secretary of the FCCDC), Charles McManus (organizer of the International Ladies Garment Workers Union), A.T. Walden (president of the Georgia Clubs and local FCCDC president), Chief W.A. Aikens, and attorney Leroy Johnson. Shown above is the front page of the *Atlanta Inquirer* on November 10, 1962.

Senator Leroy Johnson accepts a proclamation from Mayor Ivan Allen, *c.* 1960s. Leroy Johnson was elected the first African American to the state senate in 92 years from the 38th district after defeating T.M. Alexander and Rod Harris. His campaign, "A Public Record of Progress and Accomplishments," included the introduction for a public accommodation bill, a minimum wage law of $1 per hour, a statewide teacher tenure law, an anti-poll tax resolution, a change in the method of filling vacancies on the board of alderman for Atlanta, a bill to prevent furniture from being placed on the streets and sidewalks, and a bill making it easier for persons to register to vote without schooling. He led the fight to defeat an anti-picketing bill designed to prevent demonstration in Georgia and prevented three attempts to write into the new proposed state constitution a provision to prevent cities and counties from passing public accommodation ordinances over local home rule statues. During his administration, over 80 African-American boys and girls were appointed as pages in the Georgia State Capital, a first in its history. He served on the Small Loans Committee, Appropriations, Education Health and Welfare, Judiciary, and Rapid Transit. He helped to pass legislation that provided a better pension for firemen, policemen, and teachers.

When Mayor Ivan Allen was elected in 1962, he ordered the hiring of the first black firemen in the city of Atlanta. Installed on April 1, 1963, the gallant 16 were Johnny Belcher, Frank Bolden, Harvey Bowen, William Collier, Thedore Ector, William Homer, Milton Harp, Gartrell Jordan, Ralph Lester, James Maddox, Elbert Morrow, Marvin T. Reed, Quinton Redding, Harold Rosemond, Emmett Smith, and Robert Ware. The site for the Fire Station 16 was a lot on Simpson Street that had been the home of Tiger Flowers, the first African-American middleweight boxing champion in the world. The city of Atlanta acquired the property in 1962 for $25,000 and demolished the 22-room mansion for the building of the $198,000 station. The station served an area of 6 square miles and a population of 25,000. At the dedication of the site, Atlanta Life Insurance executive Jesse Hill remarked "We are witnessing more than just a dedication of a new firestation and negro firemen, we are witnessing a city growing in character, heart and spirit."

Attorneys Horace Ward and Leroy Johnson are shown taking the oath as they are sworn in the Georgia Senate, c. 1965. Ward was employed by the Hollowell-Ward law firm and qualified to seek the Democratic nomination for the 39th District seat opposing Oby T. Brewer. From 1950 to 1957, he fought to be admitted to study at the University of Georgia Law School under the guidance of Dr. William Boyd, political scientist and chairman of the Atlanta University Department of Political Science. The denial of the application by the university officials resulted in a suit in federal district court. The trial began in December 1956. The university felt that Ward was unqualified to attend because his work at Morehouse College was not accredited by SACS. After unsuccessful attempts in which Federal Judge Frank Hooper decided that the case was moot, Ward entered and finished the law school of Northwestern University in Evanston, IL, later serving in private practice and the state senate. He was appointed a federal district judge in 1979 by President Jimmy Carter.

Here, Senator Leroy Johnson entertains Robert "Bobby" Kennedy. Senator Johnson was appointed by the governor to membership on the State Democratic Executive Committee and as a delegate to the Democratic National Convention. He was also appointed by the President of the United States as a special ambassador to Zanzibar and as a member of the committee dealing with the implementation of the Civil Rights bill.

Here, the power brokers in Atlanta surround at the Atlanta Airport, including Ben Brown, Horace Ward, and Jesse Hill. Many of these men were a part of a civic group called the Atlanta Committee for Cooperative Action.

In January of 1965, eleven African Americans, including ten men and one woman, were elected to the Georgia Legislature as a result of the lower house districts being redrawn by the Georgia General Assembly. African-American state legislators on Georgia's "Capitol Hill" included, from left to right, William Alexander, Leroy Johnson, Julius Daughtery, Ben Brown, Grace Towns, Hamilton, Julian Bond, and Horace Ward.

In 1961, a young Morehouse College student, Julian Bond, attempted to integrate the visitors gallery in the Georgia State Capitol and was ejected. Five years later, at the age of 25, Julian Bond was elected to the Georgia Legislature, representing Atlanta's 136th District, defeating Rev. Howard Creecy and Malcom Dean in this newly created district. At the time of his election in 1965, Bond had attended Morehouse College and served as the communications director of the Student Non-Violent Coordinating Committee. During his campaign, he stressed more interest in the poor, as opposed to racial themes. His platform included a urban renewal program, repeal of the right to work laws, abolition of the death penalty, and removal of all voter requirements except age and residence. Bond garnered 70 percent of the primary vote and over 80 percent of the general election votes.

Julian Bond and Jesse Jackson confer in the "Black City Hall," the coffee shop of Paschal's Motor Hotel, *c.* 1970s.

In this 1972 image are officials of the Voter Education Project (VEP). Julian Bond (left) and John Lewis (right) traveled together throughout the South urging African Americans to register to vote. In 1985, the two former SNCC members would run against each other for the 5th Congressional seat of Georgia, with John Lewis winning the election in a runoff.

Mabel Sanford Lewis was a contender for the Georgia State Senate.

Benjamin D. Brown was 25 years old when he was elected to represent the 135th District of Atlanta (a substantial middle-class area) in the Georgia House of Representatives. He graduated from Clark College and the Howard University Law School and worked as the executive secretary of the Atlanta branch of the NAACP. Brown also worked as a clerk in the law firm of civil rights attorney Donald L. Hollowell.

Shown is the Clark College delegation of state officials. From left to right are Ben Brown, Julius Daughtery, Dr. Vivian Wilson Henderson (president of Clark College), and James Dean, who was elected to serve the DeKalb County District in 1969.

At the age of 34, State Representative William Alexander was elected to represent Atlanta's 133rd house district, defeating Dr. C. Clayton Powell, a African-American Republican candidate. Born in Macon, GA, Alexander, a former federal government attorney, graduated from Fort Valley State College, the University of Michigan, and Georgetown University, where he received his law degree. A veteran of the Korean War, he served as a special agent of the Counter Intelligence Corps. He ran his campaign on a platform calling for major tax reforms, criminal law reform, educational improvements, equal rights, and improved housing. He is pictured lobbying for support of his uniform crime bill in 1971.

The election of 1965 yielded great gains for African Americans in Atlanta. Dr. Horace Tate joined Dr. Rufus Clement as the second African American to serve on the Atlanta Board of Education. Ruth Sturdevant was elected to the Democratic Executive Committee with Dr. Miles Amos and Dr. Wellington Parker. There were concerns with the election of Dr. Horace Tate. Judge Sam McKenzie ruled that Tate was elected illegally to the board of education based on the fact that Tate qualified to run in the 1965 city primary after Judge Durwood Pye of the Superior Court ruled no fee could be charged to candidates to run in that primary. According to McKenzie, Tate's name should never have appeared on the primary and general election ballot. The court ruling came as a result of a suit brought by Robert S. Morely, who contended Dr. Tate did not pay a fee in qualifying as a candidate. McKenzie's ruling was later ruled illegal by the Georgia Supreme Court. Tate won the election by a majority vote in both the runoff and the general election.

In the election of 1966, 70 African Americans in Atlanta voted for gubernatorial candidate Lester Maddox, who closed his restaurant rather than serve African Americans.

In January of 1969, at a civic club luncheon, Mayor Ivan Allen, the man who spoke out in favor of the public accommodations section of the 1964 Civil Rights Act, announced that he would not seek re-election. Race relations in Atlanta still remained the city's major problem. Following the announcement, *Jet* magazine reported that black leaders were neither praising Allen or damning him. They were in a smoke-filled room somewhere in Atlanta caucusing to decide which, if any of them, had the best chance to make a winning bid to become the first black mayor of Atlanta. The statistics were simple, 46 percent of Atlanta's population was African American, but its registered voters totaled 35 percent of the city total. In order to win, a candidate would have to garner a minimum of 20 percent of the white vote, nearly 100 percent of the African-American voters would have to turn out, and the candidate would have to amass a sufficient amount of funds from the white business community to finance the campaign. Many names were tossed about including Vernon Jordan, then described as the politically ambitious director of the Southern Regional Council's Voter Education Project, Maynard Jackson, a young attorney who stirred the black voters during his spirited but unsuccessful bid to unseat Georgia senator Herman Talmedge in 1968, and State Representative Julian Bond. There was one name that stood out, the name of State Senator Leroy Johnson.

There were many political support groups, including the West Side Voters League, chaired by Milton Whote, and T.J. Curry, who served as president.

In 1968, 13 African Americans received nominations in the primary elections. They included John Hood, Charles Turner, James "Alley Pat" Patrick, Louise Watley (99th District), Rev. William Holmes Borders (107th District), Lorenzo Benn (108th District), H.L. "Hap" Hudson, attorney Leroy Johnson, attorney Horace Ward, attorney William Alexander, attorney J.C. Daugherty, Ben Brown, Julian Bond, and Grace Towns Hamilton. Two candidates with no party affiliation, Mrs. Mable Sanford Lewis and Rev. J.A. Wilborn, pastor of Union Baptist Church, were being supported by a citizens' committee in getting their names on the ballot for the 38th District against Senator Leroy Johnson.

Horace Tate, respected educator in Georgia, entered the mayoral race in 1969 ,finishing third behind Rodney Cook and Sam Massell. A few years later he was elected to the state senate in the seat once occupied by Leroy Johnson.

In 1969, attorney Maynard H. Jackson was sworn in as vice mayor by Mayor Sam Massell. In 1974, Vice Mayor jackson was elected as Atlanta's first African-American mayor.

Prominent educator and retired Morehouse College president Benjamin Elijah Mays was elected at the age of 75 as the president of the Atlanta Board of Education.

Jesse Hills, Jr., then an actuary with the Atlanta Life Insurance Company, directed the recruiting efforts for students to desegregate Georgia colleges and universities to high school students. He was also one of the founders and advisors of the *Atlanta Inquirer* newspaper. He is one of the many unsung heros of the Civil Rights Movement. In 1976, he was elected the first African-American member of the Atlanta Chamber of Commerce.

The African-American contingent of the Atlanta City Council included the following, pictured from left to right: (seated) Q.V. Williamson; (standing) James Howard, Morris Finely, Marvin Arrington, Carl Ware (elected in 1973 and served as council president from 1976 to 1979), Ira Jackson, James Bond, and John Calhoun. In 1965, following a run off, Williamson was the first African American elected to the Atlanta City Council (then Alderman's Board) since Reconstruction, defeating his white opponent, Jimmy Vickers, with 33,214 votes to 15,175. Williamson ran first in 1961, losing to Vickers. On the Alderman Board, Williamson chaired the Prison Committee and served on the Board of Firemaster, Ordinance and Legislation, and Planning and Development Committees. He was elected vice president of the board in 1969. He operated a successful real estate company located on Hunter Street. He was a native of Atlanta, born on Christmas Day in 1920, and a graduate of Booker T. Washington High School. He worked part time at Wilson Realty Company as a bookkeeper and gained the knowledge of the real estate industry. Upon graduation, he attended North Carolina A&T College before returning to complete his studies at Morehouse College. During his junior year, Dr. W.E.B. DuBois, who had heard of his exceptional office and secretarial skills, hired him and paid him twice the salary of his other two jobs. He accepted, and still maintained the other jobs. By his senior year, he had acquired his real estate brokers license. In 1941, he opened up his one-man office on Hunter Street, taught classes through the War Department and the Atlanta Board of Education, and headed the Commercial Department of Washington High School in the evenings. He was elected president of the Empire Real Estate Board and undertook a massive effort of educating the public and brokers to the complexities of urban renewal. In 1966, Williamson opened the Allen Temple apartments. He had 18 people on payroll and 20 salespeople on staff. During his last years, he chaired the Finance Committee and was instrumental in getting African Americans elected to such boards as the Joint Board of Tax Accessors, Marta, and HUD. Williamsons's term in office ended in 1981. He died on August 4, 1985. Marvin Arrington called Williamson "the Renaissance Man, a total politician."

Other African Americans serving on the city council included Joel Stokes, Arthur Langford, Henry Dodson, and Myrtle Davis. Stokes was indicted in federal court for embezzling money from Citizens Trust Bank, where he served as vice president. He was convicted in 1972 and spent 212 months in federal prison.

The first African American to serve on the Fulton County Board of Commissioners was Henry Dodson, who was elected in the 1970s.

In 1970, Andrew Young, a former lieutenant in the Southern Christian Leadership Conference, entered and won the race for the 5th Congressional seat in Congress. A graduate of Howard University and Hartford Theological Seminary, he was appointed in 1964 by Dr. Martin Luther King, Jr., to serve as executive director of SCLC.

126

Pictured are Mrs. Dorothy Bolden,
Andrew Young, and Emma Darnell.
Congressman Young was later elected
Atlanta's second African-American
mayor.

William "Bill" Campbell, after serving as
a city councilman, became the third
African-American mayor of Atlanta. He
often remarks about the historic legacy
of Atlanta's civil rights and political
communities, whose shoulders he
stands on.

BIBLIOGRAPHY

Abernathy, Ralph. *And The Walls Came Tumbling Down*. New York: Harper & Row, 1989.

Allen, Frederick. *Atlanta Rising*. Atlanta: Longstreet Press, Inc., 1996.

Chalmers, David. *Hooded Americanism* New York: Doubleday and Company, 1965.

Clayton, Xernona. *I've Been Marching All the Time*. Atlanta: Longstreet Press, 1991.

"Civil Rights Movement in the United States," Microsoft Encarta 1997 Encyclopedia. 1993–1996 Microsoft Corporation.

English, James W. *Handyman of the Lord: The Life and Ministry of Reverend William Holmes Borders*. New York: Meredith Press, 1967.

Finkelman, Paul. *Lynching, Racial Violence and Law*. New York: Garland Publishing, Inc., 1992.

Garrow, David J., Ed. *Atlanta, Georgia, 1960–1961: SitIns and Student Activism*. Atlanta: Harper & Row, Inc., 1963.

Hunter-Gault, Charlyne. *In My Place*. New York: Farrar Straus Giroux, 1992.

Lewis, John. *Walking With the Wind: A Memoir of the Movement*. New York: Simon and Schuster, c. 1998.

Mason, Herman "Skip." *Going Against The Wind: A Pictorial History of African-Americans in Atlanta*. Atlanta: Longstreet Press, c. 1992.

Muhammad, Al-Hajj Wali. *Muslims in Georgia: A Chronology and Oral History. Fayetteville*. Fayetteville, GA: The Brandon Institute, c. 1993.

Pomerantz, Gary. *Where Peachtree Meets Sweet Auburn: The Saga of Two Families and the Making of Atlanta*. New York: Scriber, 1996.

Sikes, Janice White. *Protest and Place: The Southern Civil Rights Movement, An Annotated Bibliography of Selected Resources*. Atlanta: Auburn Avenue Research Library, 1997.

Stevens, Leonard A. *Equal. The Case of Integration vs. Jim Crow*. New York: Coward, McCain and Geoghegan, 1976.

Other Sources:

Comptons Interactive Home Library 97

Encarta Encyclopedia 95

New York Public Library. 20th Century Quotations

The Afro-American

Atlanta Daily World

Atlanta Inquirer

Atlanta Journal and Constitution

Atlanta Voice

The Morris Brown College Yearbook

Other publications:

Souvenir Journal of the International Association of Black Professional Firefighters, Southeast Region Spring Conference, 1994.